Racing Towards Excellence

Demystifying the inside track to academic,
career and financial outperformance

Muzaffar Khan   Jan Sramek

Leveraged Publishing
London
2009

MUZAFFAR KHAN   JAN SRAMEK

RACING TOWARDS EXCELLENCE

DEMYSTIFYING THE INSIDE TRACK TO ACADEMIC, CAREER AND FINANCIAL OUTPERFORMANCE

First edition published in the United Kingdom in 2009 by Leveraged Publishing Ltd (Publishers).

A CIP catalogue record of this title is available from the British Library.

ISBN 978-0-9562566-0-7

Printed and bound by MPG Biddles Limited, U.K.

Cover design by Adam Baricevic.

Type set by Lukas Frelich.

Leveraged Publishing Ltd (Publishers)
36 Gilbey Road London SW17 OQF
United Kingdom

www.racing-towards-excellence.com

PEFC/16-33-293 PEFC – Promoting Sustainable Forest Management

TO OUR PARENTS

"When I was sixteen, I thought my parents knew nothing. When I was twenty-one, I was shocked to discover how much they had picked up in the last five years!"

Sir Winston Churchill, Prime Minister of the United Kingdom

Contents

Book One: Theory

Foreword

Sir Howard Davies is Director of the London School of Economics and Political Science and a member of the board of Morgan Stanley. Prior to this he was Chairman of the Financial Services Authority, the UK's financial regulator. He also served as Deputy Governor of the Bank of England and Director General of the Confederation of British Industry, and had previously worked at the Treasury, the Foreign and Commonwealth Office, and for McKinsey & Company.

Sir Howard has written two books: The Chancellors' Tales *and* Global Financial Regulation: The Essential Guide. *He holds degrees from Oxford University and the Stanford Graduate School of Business.*

A university is primarily a seat of learning, of course, but it is also a platform for self-discovery. Graduates should emerge with a good knowledge of their discipline, some useful analytical tools – which may be mathematical, psychological or even emotional – but also with a better understanding of themselves, and what they want to do with their lives.

That may seem a platitudinous observation, and indeed perhaps it is, but I am struck by how many students do not think in that way, and jump from their academic work to a career choice without reflecting hard on what they really want to do in the longer term, and on what their personal competitive advantages really are.

I confess that the above is, to a large extent, also a self diagnosis. When I was at Oxford I had little idea of what I wanted to do afterwards, or why. I chose to join the Foreign Office, largely because it was reputed to be hard to get into, and was at that time near the top of the informal pecking order of jobs, as scientifically revealed by conversations in the college bar. It also offered a way out of the Britain of 1970s, which was a depressing place. The country seemed then to be in irreversible decline. None of these reasons were good enough to sustain a career, and after two years I came to the horrible realisation that I was in the wrong place, and needed to start all over again. Luckily, I made the decisions early enough to make it possible to do so.

In recent years, it has been quite easy, especially at the LSE, for graduates to become seduced by the attractive and well paid opportunities on offer in the City of London. Why think hard about career choices when an investment bank or a management consultancy is prepared to flatter your ego and send you a fancy offer accompanied by a magnum of champagne in an elegant padded box?

Jan Sramek and Muzaffar Khan have themselves received such tempting offers in the past. So they know the game from personal experience. They are well placed to explain how to maximise your chances, if that is what you want. But the big point I draw from what they have written is that it can make sense to take a much broader view of personal development than students typically take. They offer an interesting taxonomy – the 'four accounts framework' – which can help you think through your own strengths and weaknesses, and how to maximise the former while offsetting the latter as far as possible.

Every reader will, I am sure, take something different away from the book. My own favourite piece of advice, which feeds a prejudice of mine, is in the section on *How to think outside the box*. The first point there, is very simple: *"read a lot"*. That is something I have done throughout my life, and never regretted it.

I am often depressed by how reluctant students are to read outside their discipline, or even outside that week's essay topic. Jan is surely right when he says that *"reading books is like cheating – you are getting advice on life experience from some of the greatest minds of humanity"*. And I would emphasise that that can include works of fiction as well. There is nothing like a good novel to allow you to imagine different experiences, different lives.

Others will certainly find different points at which to connect with the book, and will be stimulated by other arguments and recommendations in what is a very rich and clear text. I hope it achieves a wide audience.

Howard Davies

Introduction

How this book came about, and why we wrote it.

The life of young people around the world has become more complicated in the past two decades. The pressure is on: expectations are increasing and the race for children to outperform and succeed in life starts earlier than ever before. Increased access to education and career opportunities has been one of the greatest benefits of the wealth creation that took place across the world in the last two decades. It also means, however, that today's young generations are growing up in an environment that is much more highly pressured than the one in which their parents or grandparents grew up.

Unfortunately, the teaching of life skills[1] required to succeed in this new competitive landscape has, in general, not kept up with the developments. Our schools and universities focus primarily on academic disciplines and rigorous scientific analysis. Consequently, the students have to take responsibility to prepare for the other challenges of life and work themselves – a difficult task at that age. The outcome is inevitable. High expectations, both of the individuals and those around them, collide with a lack of relevant preparation and result in unhappiness.

> The World Health Organization has defined life skills as *"abilities for adaptive and positive behaviour that enable individuals to deal effectively with the demands and challenges of everyday life"*. In particular, life skills are a group of cognitive, personal and interpersonal abilities that

> help people make informed decisions, solve problems, think critically and creatively, communicate effectively, build healthy relationships, empathise with others, and cope with and manage their lives in a healthy and productive manner.
>
> UNESCO
>
> Please refer to Appendix A for the full explanation of life skills.

It is universities and employers across the world that eventually face the consequences of these problems. Too often, students and recent graduates are either relaxed and happy, or successful, but rarely both. This is illustrated by numerous cases of burn-outs on the one hand and drop-outs on the other. It is unfortunate, though understandable, that only a small proportion of students and graduates succeed in finding the elusive 'work-life' balance, and outperform in a way that leads to happiness. Why? Nobody has ever taught the majority of them how to do it.

We have written this book to fill the gap. Having worked together in a mentor-mentee relationship for almost two years and having both individually outperformed in different areas in life, we believe that sharing our accumulated knowledge and experience will help others better understand the factors that drive success. We hope that the small nudges in the right direction, contained in this book, will be like the proverbial few snowflakes that unleash an avalanche.

Muzaffar Khan (40) retired from a successful career on Wall Street and became Vice-Chairman of an international environmental charity. In 2007, whilst completing his MSc degree at the London School of Economics, he gave a series of lectures on life skills. It was then that he met Jan Sramek, at the time a 2nd year undergraduate who had shown great promise in academia, financial markets and entrepreneurship. Muzaffar became one of Jan's mentors, and the relationship has since contributed to Jan's accelerating outperformance.

It quickly became clear that learning life skills makes a significant difference to young people's success and happiness, if introduced sufficiently early. Realising this, we set out to write this book together and combine theory with practical skills and implementation, as well as combining the perspectives of a teacher and a student.

What is this book about and what will it do for me?

This book explains how and when outperformance happens, how it creates a virtuous cycle with happiness and how to achieve both in practice. Remarkably, outperforming in different disciplines requires surprisingly similar skills and ways of thinking. The framework we present is therefore applicable to any field or activity, including academia, business, entrepreneurship, finance, sports, arts and so on.

Book One, Theory, lays the foundations of outperformance and the value system that makes it one and the same with happiness. Chapter 1, Four Accounts, introduces the principle of a balanced approach to life. The next few chapters are designed to show how to progress from the original inspiration to a place of self-respect and self-confidence. Chapter 2, Inspiration, describes what motivates and inspires us, and rigorously examines enthusiasm, the fuel of success for the outperformer. Chapter 3, Vision, talks about differences between objectives and vision, and explains the difference between the life strategies of under- and out-performers. Chapter 4, Love, relates outperformance to our relationships – both to ourselves and to others. Finally, Chapter 5, Responsibility, re-defines the way we think about responsibility towards ourselves and others, and helps to put things into context.

Book Two, Practice, has twelve chapters. Chapter 6, Measurability and Yardsticks, describes how outperformers monitor their progress, and why such monitoring is important. Chapter 7, Habits, talks about our habits, why they are important and how to change them. Chapter 8, Drive, describes how to create inspiration in a very practical way. Chapter 9, Doing What You Love, explains how to discover what you love and sustain your motivation. Chapter 10, Health and Fitness, looks into the importance of these issues for the outperformer and specifically outlines best practices for diet, sleep and exercise. Chapter 11, Communication, explains the most common problems in this area, and how to prevent them. Chapter 12, Relationships and Networking, offers practical guidance on what defines healthy relationships and how to create them. Chapter 13, Mentors and Buddies, explains the importance of these relationships and suggests how to find the right ones. Chapter 14, Racing Against Time, explains the importance of time as a commodity, and suggests how to become more efficient. Chapter 15, Study Skills, offers proven strategies for learning effectively and doing well in exams. Chapter 16, Thinking Outside the Box, explains this concept and offers ways of using it to sharpen your mind, as well as some of its practical applications. Chapter 17, Productive Leisure, identifies reasons why many young people waste their free time in an unproductive way, and offers suggestions for change.

By the time you finish reading this book, you should be able to answer the following questions.

1. What is outperformance, and how and when does it happen?

2. How are happiness and outperformance related, and why does the former lead to the latter?

3. How do you identify what you really enjoy, become inspired by it, and create your life vision?

4. How do you live a life focused on achieving this vision while being happy?

5. How do you develop the skills required for achieving your vision, and how do you execute all of our strategies?

The gap in the knowledge of life skills that we wish to fill exists across all schools, universities and employers to a degree. Our aim is to level the playing field, allow everyone to maximise the opportunities they have been given, and help them create new ones. This applies especially to those who have not had access to the best schools, universities and mentors. It is our belief in your ability to achieve extraordinary things if you work hard and smart that we want to convey to you throughout this book. We hope to support young people in their ability to think outside the box, leave the herd-mentality behind and start thinking for themselves.

The book will constantly switch between he and she when talking about outperformers. This is deliberate. Success and happiness are genderless aspirations and our teachers in this arena hail from both genders.

Muzaffar Khan: Reconciliation

"Having known Muzaffar for as long as I have, I can say that he is the living demonstration of the application of 'Life Skills'. He has shown by his life that no matter what obstacle or circumstance one faces, anyone with the correct approach can rise above any situation and win the day, and also maintain the ideals that all great philosophers talk about."

Marc Cheval
Portfolio Manager, Moore Capital Management
previously Managing Director, Goldman Sachs

In 2003 I was at Moore Europe Capital Management, one of the world's largest hedge funds. Two of the three senior members of my team had joined in September 1997; I arrived four months later. I had five years of stimulating experiences and learnt a great deal. Just as importantly, I had started out with two colleagues and ended up with two friends.

Given my earlier stints at Citibank and Barclays Capital, I had been, by any measure, blessed with a successful career in investment banking and the hedge fund world. I was in contact with finance ministries and central banks around the globe and travelled from Budapest to Buenos Aires to Beijing.

And then I resigned. I felt unfulfilled and left to become Vice-Chairman of ACOPS, an international environmental charity. Why did I feel this way? At the time, I was not sure myself.

A few months after leaving Moore Capital I visited Tibet where I met some remarkable individuals who urged me to become more self-reflective about my life choices, and the subconscious reasons that led to them. I worked with various teachers over the next few years, delving deeper into many areas of behavioural psychology, theology, and many esoteric teachings. Having studied these areas before when coaching others and helping them succeed, the focus was, for the first time, on me, and unlocking what made me happy and why. I could not have foreseen the answers.

I realised that from an early age the idea was ingrained in me that with privilege and power comes the obligation to help others. My obligations were broken down for me into three distinct areas:

1. To look after my parents and grandparents when I became an adult.
2. As the eldest son, to look after my three younger brothers.
3. To make a positive contribution to humanity.

What was interesting about my upbringing was that no one inculcated in me a desire to be either happy or successful. Success was assumed and happiness was seen as a natural outcome of meeting my obligations. It is only now, in my forties, that I have learnt, and maybe why I so passionately teach, that this is exactly the wrong way round.

My upbringing had a significant effect on my activities both before I started on Wall Street and during my career there. From when my two brothers, ten and twelve years younger than me, came to study in England in 1992, I had always been their guardian. My parents paid all our school fees, but remained in Pakistan and so the oversight of my brothers passed to me. I still consider it one of my greatest contributions that I helped them achieve higher grades in their undergraduate degrees than I did. The joy I felt from their success has been a huge inspiration to increase my commitment to mentoring others to excel.

Between university and Citibank, I spent a few years working for charities and being a carer for my grandfather, who had suffered from Parkinson's disease for 30 years. Even after joining Wall Street, I continued contributing to society in different ways. I mentored younger colleagues and people from the industry, and coached young students from my community. What is interesting is that despite my extensive involvement with charitable activities before Moore Capital, I still felt that I needed further justification for success beyond meeting obligations 1 and 2 above.

It became apparent after Tibet that the charitable and mentoring activities had been attempts to reconcile my closely held beliefs, instilled in me by my parents, with my success. Contributing unconditionally to others was the only activity that I knew made me happy, as only then did I feel that I deserved success.

Unearthing these answers made sense of a lot of things, and I felt a deep sense of peace. Knowing why I had made my choices allowed me to become a much better teacher to my students. I could now help them deconstruct their motivations and psychological biases. The resulting clarity allowed my students and I to strategise for both happiness and success. At this time more senior executives from different industries started to approach me for coaching.

It is not a coincidence that it now became possible to see my own path to happiness and success. I met Stanley Fink who was at the time CEO of Man Group Plc, an asset management firm overseeing $75 billion. Stanley was effortlessly implementing the teachings that I had just learned. He loved his job, and as a consequence, was very good at it. This, in turn, allowed him to raise millions of dollars for charities he cared about every year.

Stanley's next ambition was combining his passions for finance and the environment, previously inconceivable. At the time, I was just finishing my second postgraduate degree, specialising in development and environmental finance at the LSE. Stanley invited me to become a consultant for Man Group in 2006, and I saw him initiate a multimillion dollar business within the firm which specialised in creating solutions to environmental problems, thereby reconciling his passion and his skills. By the time both he and I left the company in 2008, a business had been created that was successfully capturing methane emissions from Chinese coal mines.

It was my time with Man Group that inspired me to reconcile my passions with my skills. Outlining what makes this book different explains why I asked Jan to write it with me.

What makes this book different?

We empathically address 18–25 year olds. We grow and develop as we get older. We are not the same people aged 40 that we were at 30. In particular, we tend to change a lot faster in our teens and twenties than later on in life. It is therefore surprising that to our knowledge, no holistic books on the subject of outperformance have been written for university students and recent graduates. In addition, there certainly does not seem to be any work published by someone from this age group, for this age group.

We write about clearly defined goals and how to measure them. This is not a book about how to become happy in life and reach peace with oneself in some abstract, esoteric way. We use many abstract, esoteric concepts, but the purpose of this book is to help you lead a happy life through clearly defined outperformance in the key areas of your personal development – emotional, material, mental and physical.

We explain in detail why we use these areas and how they produce outperformance and, in turn, happiness. We also describe how to measure and increase them in the most efficient, practical and leveraged way, and how they are interconnected.

We focus on the low-hanging fruit. The Pareto principle, also known as the 80/20 rule, suggests that 20% of our efforts are responsible for 80% of our success. The principle has been observed empirically and relevant strategies implemented across a number of different fields, including marketing, sales, research, innovation, sport, start-up companies and engineering.[2]

We have identified a number of skills and concepts that tend to be responsible for the large majority of gains and improvements for outperformers. This work is based on experience, research and observation. We show throughout this book that, surprisingly, you only need to get a relatively small number of things right in your thinking and behaviour in order to outperform. The focus on picking this low-hanging fruit distinguishes this book from others.

We focus on efficiency, conciseness and depth of research. We understand that you live busy lives in a busy world. This book is designed to be concise, to the point and with immediate added value. It gives you a broad overview of many areas of self improvement. At the same time, this is a densely researched book which provides a substantial number of references if you wish to comprehensively study any particular area. The intention is to give you the maximum possible benefit whilst taking the least possible amount of your time.

We combine theory and practice. There are a number of great books on the theory of personal development. There are also a number of great books on the practical aspects of this subject. There are very few books that manage to combine the two areas successfully – yet this is, in our opinion, where the real change happens.

One of the most powerful concepts introduced in this book is that of virtuous and vicious circles of out- or under-performance. One can, however, only take advantage of these ideas by combining the understanding of the theoretical framework and the practical advice. Furthermore, the combination of the two makes it easier to achieve and recognise immediate tangible results.

In many ways, this book is an attempt to correct certain detrimental biases and decision making failures. These biases and failures occur as a consequence of behavioural, psychological, sociological and environmental influences. In fact, one of the major roles of the theoretical part is to explain and correct these in a way that allows the mind to accept the logic of the corrections. Our hope is that you will often experience a 'eureka' moment and relate what you read to your experience and experience of others around you.

This book has been written by two people who have worked together in a mentor/mentee relationship. Combining our different experiences, insights and understanding of what drives outperformance has helped us to write a book of very condensed life skills advice. Furthermore, we believe that our cooperation to date has allowed us to structure its content in a way that is most natural and helpful for anyone trying to implement it. It is based on our life experience and interaction with outperformers, as well as my decade-long coaching experience. It contains a collection of best practices that lead to outperformance.

Working with Jan reminds me of my work with Stanley Fink. Like Stanley, he has always followed the principles from the beginning. Jan has the same look on his face when I am unveiling a theory, which I have spent years researching and teaching, and consider a great insight, but which is second nature to him. That is why he is the perfect partner for explaining the strategies. He has lived them consistently and naturally.

Jan Sramek: A Leveraged Life

"We need to internalize this idea of excellence. Not many folks spend a lot of time trying to be excellent."

Barack Obama, 44th President of the United States

The last five years have been very good to me. I scored ten A grades at A-level and three Distinctions at S-level, was named *Olympic Hope* in handball and have been awarded almost £100,000 in scholarships by academic and financial institutions. I have interned in trading and research at some of the world's major investment banks (Goldman Sachs, Barclays Capital, UBS and Deutsche Bank) and hedge funds (Marshall Wace Asset Management and AKO Capital). I have been named a 'wildcard entry' onto the nomination list of the *Top 100 Rising Stars of European Financial Markets* by Financial News, selected as *One To Watch* by university peers, and been interviewed by CNN and several national newspapers.

Along the way, I have founded and run four companies involved in social networking, graduate recruitment, West End night-club promotion and university admissions training. I have also founded a successful charity focusing on levelling out the playing field for applicants to Oxford and Cambridge. Right now I am revising for my finals, about to finish my undergraduate degree at the LSE, having transferred here two years ago from Trinity College, Cambridge in order to leverage my two greatest passions: financial markets and entrepreneurship.

But I came from a very different world. I grew up living in one room with my parents and a younger brother, in my grand-mother's house, the last one on top of a hill, next to a forest, in a village of 1,000 people in the middle of Moravia, in Eastern Europe. I am only the second person in my extended family to attend university, and the first one to have studied or worked abroad.

My success has been significantly accelerated by specific relationships and ideas that leveraged my natural ability into far greater outperformance than would have otherwise been the case. Seeing the progression from where I started in life to where I am today, I believe it is important to share my journey and show that there is nothing unique about what I have done that could not be implemented by you.

Early childhood (1987 – 1998)

I was born in 1987 in the Czech Republic under a communist regime. My father worked for Czech Radiocommunications as a technician, having trained as a car mechanic and had never graduated from high school. My mother was a primary school teacher; she studied Russian at university.

My father worked in Prague, 250 kilometres away, and stayed there every week from Sunday to Thursday. My first memories are of Thursday afternoons – I would stand in my cot and impatiently wait for the door bell announcing my father's arrival. Having spent hours on trains and buses, he would come directly to the bedroom and sit with me for hours, answering my questions about why planes fly, how you drill for oil and so on while my mother waited with his dinner. She started her second degree shortly after my brother was born in 1988, and so my father would spend the rest of the week taking me and my brother for walks in the woods so that my mother could study.

It is to the endless patience of both of my parents that I attribute my early and rapid intellectual development. They must have spent hundreds of hours of quality time with me – they told me stories, played games with me, taught me arithmetic, how to play sports and how to run. My father would often bring home mechanical components or motors, take them apart with me and explain how the different parts worked together. It was my parents' dedication to treating me as an equal, according to my ability rather than age, and developing my curiosity and intellect that I believe ignited what later became a talent and interest in natural sciences, and mathematics in particular. It gave me an expectation that I would understand things, a sense of confidence and a desire to be treated like an adult all the time; these have served me well in life many times since then.

Then came 1989 and the (non-violent) Velvet Revolution which saw the overthrow of the Communist government. While this did not change my day-to-day life at the time, forces were set in motion that would create the opportunities I capitalised on much later.

In 1990, my parents started reconstructing my father's old house in another small village (this time of 1,600 people), some 75 kilometres away from where we lived. One day my parents let me play on a lawn next to the house where a group of builders had started construction of a new workshop. Having seen them build the entire structure up to the roof, this confident little three year old innocently asked, much to their shock and amusement, about where the windows were going to be. It turned out that in their over-confidence, they did not care to look at the plans and forgot about leaving space for windows. Fortunately, the early question gave them enough time to take the bricks apart and make the appropriate changes.

We moved into our new house in 1991 and my mother went back to work, accepting a teaching post at a high school in a nearby town. My father had by then left his previous company and set up on his own, becoming a self-employed technician of back-up electricity diesel-generators, something he has done ever since.

I started attending the local kindergarten, and moved into a primary school two years later. By indulging my natural curiosity, my parents had helped me develop multiple skills and talents, and I immediately became the top student in the class. I was lucky to be growing up in a country where the educational system catered to different intelligences from very early on. From day one we were taught a broad range of subjects, including mathematics, natural sciences, biological sciences, history, geography, Czech language and literature, music, art and so on.

What was remarkable during those formative years of my life was my parents ability to create an inspiring environment where outperformance was natural, rather than expected. The pressure was non-existent, replaced by an almost implicit understanding that I would go on to do great things. Although this has remained important to me, I believe it was those early days when it really made a difference. I started seeing success as natural and behaving accordingly.

My parents' thinking on parenting and education – extremely progressive for the time and place – has played a similarly important role. My chores as a child were very light to non-existent, as was any intervention from either of them into how I spent my free time. This allowed me to spend much of it studying what I wanted to study, rather than what others thought I should study.

Between the ages of seven and twelve, it was reading. I developed a habit of reading the leading broadsheets cover to cover, and quickly became obsessed with following both local and international economics, business and politics. Fiction took centre stage though, and Arthur C. Clarke, Isaac Asimov, Jules Verne and many others played a central part in shaping my perception of the world at the time. I joined the local handball club and started developing a passion for a sport that would play a significant role in my life later on.

Having spent three years at the local school, I realised that I needed better teaching. Once again, my parents took my views seriously and considered them on merit rather than my age, transferring me to a different school in a town nearby. I was lucky that my new teachers recognised and supported my talents, and I could spend classes working independently through more advanced material. I won my first Maths Olympiad.

It was clear when I started fifth grade that the next logical step was to apply for a selective eight year programme for high achieving students. These were run by grammar schools and took their students all the way to A-levels. I applied to the best grammar school in my region, and topped the entrance exam.

I did not know it then but it was my parents who gave me the three year advantage in key skills of reasoning and mathematics, and thereby created the great game-changing relationship during this period. They also gave me the confidence to believe in my own opinions, voice them and stand up for them, even when my views differed from the consensus.

Secondary school (1998 – 2004)

I was lucky to grow up in a society where the quality of schooling one receives depends purely on merit and where talent is identified and developed very early on. I quickly made use of the opportunities available at the new school, immediately becoming the top of my class and continued to win prizes in Mathematics, Physics and Informatics Olympiads. This in turn won me invitations to attend regular seminars on mathematics with university professors, further accelerating my progress in the subject.

It was the internet, however, that would fundamentally change my life over the next few years. In 1997, my parents decided to spend a substantial part of their total income on buying a personal computer – not for my father's business, or my mother's work, but purely so that my brother and I could go and explore.

My interest started with pure curiosity but I quickly moved on to learning programming, databases etc. Shortly afterwards, I accepted a promising offer from an IT magazine, and started writing technical articles on a freelance basis. My articles immediately received the highest rankings of all published pieces, and became the most widely read part of the magazine.

When I realised that there was a shortage of skilled professionals on the market, I began developing bespoke website and database solutions for small and medium-sized enterprises – aged 13. This created a big leap in my maturity – in addition to having serious responsibility, dealing with clients and the business side of things, I started making money. Not a small amount, either – my income was higher than that of my teachers.

I used a part of that income to start betting on sports. As well as being the first proper experience involving money and risk, this gave me a business idea. I realised that there was a lack of high quality sports statistics providers on the market. At the same time, online betting was expanding, creating opportunities to make money from advertising. I launched the business together with a school friend in early 2001. Obviously I could not found the company aged 13, so my mother agreed to set it up for me in her name. The site quickly took off, and went on to win a *Young Entrepreneur* prize from the Ministry of Informatics, following a project of mine that had won a year earlier and making me one of only two people who had received the award twice.

Though I did not see it then, this gave me the social status and credibility needed for a venture that brought broadband into the village where we lived. By the end of 2003, I had grown frustrated with the expensive and slow dial-up connection – there were no alternatives. Deciding that there had to be a way, I contacted all ISP providers nearby, and asked them about the subsidies they would need to take this, otherwise commercially non-viable, project forward. I got their requirements, pitched the idea to the Mayor and Local Council, and convinced them to back and fund the project. I negotiated an attractive commission scheme with the chosen provider, and helped them with the set up and marketing.

By this time, we were performing against all odds in handball. Though we were a small team from a small village, we were beating clubs from major cities. I had become one of the best players and scorers in the entire league, and fell in love with the sport, training many hours outside of the scheduled times. Then came an invitation for the *Olympics Hopes* team selection camp. I made it through, and got head-hunted by one of the four 'sports centres of youth' to join the fast-track programme. The offer involved signing a professional contract, relocating and training for the highest European competitions and the national team.

I wanted to go, at any cost. At 14, I was marginally more idealistic and stubborn than I am today, but the head-hunters needed my parents to sign off the transfer. I thought it was a formality, but my father said "No.", for the first and last time in my life. I could argue, sulk, threaten, nothing would change his mind. He had decided that my talents could be used better elsewhere and did not relent even when they tried to bribe him. We did not speak for weeks. I only realised that he was right, and had probably saved my career, several months later.

One of the things that shaped both my life and my thinking at the time started as a seemingly unproductive addiction. I started playing a text-based online strategic fantasy game, which within days became a complete obsession. The game was played by over 10,000 players at the time but an elite few controlled the top ranks. I broke that glass ceiling within weeks, the first newbie to ever do so, and went on to spend days of my time leading one of the largest alliances, and later on becoming a member of the management team.

We were obsessed. It was quite normal to receive a call at 3am in the morning from one of your allies asking you to log in and do something. We left school classes, business meetings, even dates with various excuses. As unlikely as it sounds, however, I have learnt a great deal about strategy, leadership and people from this experience. I only found out much later the identities of my co-players who turned out to be leading entrepreneurs, scientists, university professors, managers and politicians. Somewhere along the way, I scored 13 A*s in the Czech GCSE-equivalent.

The internet fundamentally changed my life in many ways. It created equality of information access with my peers in the most advanced economies in the world, across all income and age groups. It provided material benefits and access to new business opportunities with low barriers to entry. Last but not least, it was the internet that brought me to the UK.

In 2003, I randomly stumbled upon an online advertisement for a scholarship scheme for high schools students interested in spending one year in the United Kingdom. The scheme was run by the *Open Society Foundation*, George Soros' vehicle for change in the world. I applied, went through multiple rounds of tests and interviews, and was selected for the scheme from several hundred applicants from across the country. The internet not only gave me the information that opened me up to the idea of studying in the west, it also helped me find the resources to do so.

United Kingdom (2004 – 2009)

I arrived by bus at the Victoria coach station, London in September 2004. Having never visited an English speaking country before and with a modest command of the language,

I was thrown in. After a few days of an introduction course in Cambridge, I arrived at Bootham School, York and began a very different part of my life.

Bootham for me was really about fantastic teachers who were equally amazing people. It is difficult to describe just how much that place has changed my life. For one, my scholarship was only for one year, and the intention was that I would go back to the Czech Republic and finish my studies there afterwards. Bootham generously offered me a full scholarship for the second year – without their support, my family could never have paid for my education.

Seeing my passion and interest for the subjects, my teachers put no limits on their time or dedication to push me further. I started with six subjects, picking up one more at the beginning of my second year. Next came an argument with friends over the difficulty of A-levels and a bet which resulted in me picking up three further subjects a few weeks before my final exams, as well as three advanced S-papers.

I remain grateful to this day for all the support and patience with scheduling Bootham provided at the time. In a marathon of over 78 hours of exams, including days when I had to be supervised overnight, I sat 44 papers that summer, breaking all existing records. I scored ten A's at A-levels, gaining 100% in over half of the papers and a 96% average overall, as well as three Distinctions at S-level. The story was broadcast by TV, radio and newspapers. It was an interesting challenge, as was fencing, swimming and other sports I played at school. The most defining aspect of Bootham, however, was definitely its success in creating, once again in my life, an environment where success was natural, rather than demanded or expected.

I went on to study Mathematics on a full scholarship at Trinity College, Cambridge. In the summer before university, I founded Oxbridge-Admissions.info, a charity aimed at levelling out the playing field for applicants to Oxford and

Cambridge. Today, we provide nearly 1,000 profiles of both successful and unsuccessful candidates and have helped over 100,000 potential applicants from all over the world.

In Cambridge, I enjoyed both my courses and the non-academic side of university life, including the opportunity to start pursuing my interest in financial markets and entre-preneurship on a more serious level. I completed a number of spring and summer internships in trading with investment banks, including Goldman Sachs, Barclays Capital, UBS and Deutsche Bank. I won the Cambridge round of a trading game organised by Citigroup, and made it to the national final. I applied for, and won, the UBS Academic Scholarship, one of the most prestigious awards for first year undergraduates.

I founded Nicube Ltd, a company which helps students choose their careers and make them happen, and started working on CrewDates, an innovative platform that 'makes making friends easy'. Several months later, we were funded by an angel investor and the idea turned into a business, CrewDates Limited.

I joined the First & Third Trinity Boat Club and rowed in the sixth seat of the first novice eight, started shooting, renewed my interest in ballroom dancing and got elected as the Vice-President of the Cambridge University Investment Club. Within two months, we raised the Club's budget fivefold and significantly expanded its operations, making it the most advanced student-run investment fund in Europe. I later set up and co-ran the Club's macro trading strategy, and became its Chief Investment Officer. Having been elected as the Junior Treasurer of the First & Third Trinity Boat Club May Ball, I leveraged my contacts in the City to raise our sponsorship budget.

It was after my internship in Fixed Income Trading at Barclays Capital in the summer after my first year that I took one of the most radical decisions in my life. In a sudden burst of clarity,

I realised that despite all of the great things about Cambridge, if my interests were really in finance and entrepreneurship, it was not the right place for me. I took my chances and contacted the London School of Economics about a possible transfer. I was very lucky to be heard by the right people in the Mathematics department, who kindly listened to my case, took a risk with me and found a way to facilitate my transfer into the second year of the School's BSc Mathematics and Economics programme.

Leaving Trinity was not easy, and I had to leave behind a full scholarship at the college. Fortunately, the award I had received earlier from UBS allowed me to finance my education in London. My parents were understandably shocked when they heard about my transfer ... particularly given that it was not until a few weeks into Michaelmas term that I told them about it. It took me months to convince them of its merit.

Transferring to the LSE significantly accelerated my personal development. The School had the perfect mix of people, opportunities, environment and location for my work in financial markets and entrepreneurship. It was in the summer between Cambridge and LSE that I met Muzaffar Khan, the co-author of this book. We both quickly understood that our personality mix was an interesting one, similar in many ways but very different in others, and started a mentor-mentee relationship that resulted in writing this book together. Our work helped me clarify and systemise many of the ideas and principles I had been intuitively following before. This, in turn, allowed me to accelerate my progress even further.

Much happened during the following two years. I started working part-time as an Investment Analyst at AKO Capital, a hedge fund. I helped Marshall Wace, another hedge fund, create a scholarship programme; I later became one of the scholars and interned with the firm in Quantitative Trading and Research. I went back to Goldman Sachs and completed a second internship on the firm's trading desks in Emerging

Markets and Commodities. I ended up being headhunted by some of the world's largest hedge funds during my final year at university.

I was asked to give lectures on trading and financial markets at LSE, Imperial College London, University College London and City University. My peers and the recruitment agency FreshMinds chose me as a *One To Watch*. I am the youngest person ever to be nominated to the list of *Top 100 Rising Stars of European Financial Markets* by Financial News. Deciding to broaden my understanding of financial markets, I started studying for, and successfully completed, the first level of the Chartered Financial Analyst programme. The Gateway, UK's national student newspaper, profiled me as a 'Tycoon of Tomorrow'.

My entrepreneurial ventures significantly benefited from relocating to London. I developed and expanded Nicube into a knowledge base for students and junior professionals with interest to work in the City. We launched CrewDates in Oxford and Cambridge, and started preparing a launch in London this summer. I became a Partner at AlphaParties Ltd, a West End nightclub entertainment business. Finally, I put together a team that is running Sucedo Ltd, a business focused on providing first class preparation to foreign candidates applying to UK's leading universities.

I also became heavily involved within the LSE itself. I am an adviser on hedge funds to the LSE Alternative Investments Conference and have joined several of the School's internal committees. Based on my experience in online business, I have helped and advised the LSE on its public relations, information policy, internal blogs and a planned new website. I supported the LSE entrepreneurial internships scheme, and hired a few students to work for my companies, as well as helping the Careers Service provide new insights into recruitment to the biggest graduate recruiters. I became one of the selected finalists to write about their experience on the

LSE Finalists blog, and represented the school in a students' debate aired by CNN. I achieved a First in my second year exams.

Great teachers, managers, and mentors had taken on the role previously provided by my parents and the internet. I could not have done ten A-levels without support from my teachers at Bootham. I could not have transferred to the LSE without a buy-in from the Mathematics department, as well as my former professors at Cambridge. My steep learning curve in trading and research has been accelerated by a number of fantastic managers, mentors and colleagues who shared their time and insight with a young intern, just because they saw and believed in my potential.

Finally, it was my work with Muzaffar that helped me deconstruct and understand my outperformance to date, and bring increased clarity to my thinking. Furthermore, our work on reframing everything in terms of symbiotic relationships with others and the environment has once again clarified what was previously subconscious. It has outlined why and how success and human values are not incompatible.

Over the last two years, I have seen many of my own mentees accelerate their success and go on to do great things. When Muzaffar suggested we leverage our insights by writing a book that could address a much broader audience than we could hope to reach individually, I immediately bought into the idea.

I am about to start a new period of my life and join Goldman Sachs as an Emerging Markets Trader in July 2009. This book is my way of contributing to my generation in the same leveraged way that certain relationships have contributed to my life.

As you turn the page and start the first chapter, I offer one piece of advice: approach everything we say with an open mind, and do not judge our strategies before you try them, or at least before you reach the end of the book. I have lived them my entire life, intuitively or consciously. Trust me, they work.

Book One
Theory

Chapter 1
The Four Accounts

"Olympism ... exalting and combining in a balanced whole the qualities of body, mind and will."

Pierre de Coubertin, founder of the Modern Olympics

"People with great gifts are easy to find, but symmetrical and balanced ones never."

Ralph Waldo Emerson, philosopher and poet

1.1 What are the Four Accounts?

The concept of the Four Accounts is our framework for looking at performance and happiness. There are four separate areas of a human being's personal assets that allow him or her to function in today's society. These are (in alphabetical order):

- Emotional health[3]
- Material wealth[4]
- Mental health[5]
- Physical health[6]

You have to invest in each of these four areas in order to create happiness; these four parts of your life need a basic level of a positive balance for you to survive, but a higher level is needed in order to reach what we would call happiness.

1.2 Why are the Four Accounts important?

Because each account requires a positive balance for survival, the Four Accounts are each individually important, but together they represent everything that is important for happiness. If any one of your accounts falls close to zero, you stop functioning independently. If you are too unhealthy, too depressed, too poor, or too ignorant, it is impossible to look after yourself, let alone be happy.

Of course, different people have different preferences, and hence the desirable 'distribution' of their total 'health and wealth' between the Four Accounts will be unique to them. Extreme cases, however, tend not to produce happiness.

An example of this would be many executives, both male and female, who have failed marriages behind them or who do not have the kind of relationships – mutually nurturing and respectful – that they would like to have with their children. These emotional costs often lead to burn-outs or at least regret and almost never produce happiness. If you are hurting on the inside because you have no stable emotional relationships or you feel rejected for who you are by other people, this will most likely lead to paranoia and depression. A nervous breakdown cannot lead to happiness regardless of how much money you have.[7]

If you do not have enough money to feed yourself and your family properly, as is too often the case in third world countries, you cannot be happy. Food, shelter and clothing are basic human needs. Many psychologists and motivational theorists have shown that human happiness increases when a basic minimum of these are met. Reports of global poverty-fighting charities provide a wealth of empirical evidence for this thesis.[8]

Great unhappiness due to inadequate financial means can and does arise even in the developed world. The people who lived on excessive credit over the last decade are now facing foreclosure on their homes. Many of them will most likely see their real living standards fall for several years, particularly in the US and the UK. Such events will generally produce unhappiness. At the extreme, the psychological effects of bankruptcy have been well documented by researchers, e.g. in the United States and in the United Kingdom.

Consider the lawyers and bankers who traded their health (or what we would call physical account) in exchange for material gains.[9] We have yet to meet a single person who, having suffered through a heart attack or other debilitating illnesses would not have chosen a different strategy. No amount of wealth can compensate if one ends up being bedridden.

Finally, inadequate focus on the mental account can lead to unhappiness both directly and indirectly through its impact on the other three accounts. Lack of basic education creates significant challenges to finding an interesting job, integrating oneself in society and developing healthy habits. Adult ignorance, often the conscious decision to deny oneself access to knowledge, can have a negative impact on the individual, both in terms of his ability to utilise opportunities and to make well informed decisions.

1.3 Why are the Four Accounts a good way of thinking about personal growth?

There are two fundamental reasons for using the Four Accounts:

Firstly, they together create a balanced, happy human being.

Secondly, they are easily measurable.

There are many other theories that meet the first criterion – of creating a balanced, happy human being. The key contribution and uniqueness of the Four Accounts concept comes from its second property – measurability.

This property makes it easier to track and evaluate progress, and feel satisfaction from improved performance. A theory with no quantifiable benchmarks can at best address only one half of our brain – the right one. Our right (emotional) brain[10] can emotionally feel value[11] for anything; our left (logical) brain, however, cannot see anything that is not measurable as having value. The Four Accounts address this problem.

- You know that your physical account is increasing if you are running faster or lifting more weights than last month.

- The material account is easy to measure; if your total assets are greater now than they were yesterday then an increase in the material account has occurred.

- A good way of measuring improvements in your emotional account is to see if the diversity and depth of your relationships is increasing.

- Finally, if your performance in exams or tests improves, or you start reading more books, then your mental account is increasing.

1.4   Do the Four Accounts actually work?

One should not forget that the Four Accounts are just a model; like any model, it is to be evaluated on the basis of its power to explain and predict reality, rather than its elegance. We would encourage you to apply this framework to people in your own lives, and see for yourself whether it works or not.

To give some examples, it is perhaps worth looking at stories of four people who seem to be very focused on their Four Accounts, and who have undoubtedly outperformed in the world.

Bill Gates

Bill Gates started out very much focused on the mental account – he went to Harvard. He then quickly moved onto the material account by starting and growing Microsoft. Recently, however, he has also been making sure that his material success and mental prowess bring him emotional satisfaction.

In particular, starting a healthcare and education-based charity with his wife – the Bill and Melinda Gates Foundation – is an excellent example of sharing a philanthropic cause with one's partner. Gates is, according to himself, happily married. Both he and his wife appear to be very physically fit and relaxed.

The combination of the four – the looking after himself, the emotional focus, the earlier mental and material focus – has today created a person who is widely respected:

"I meet many high net-worth individuals that are watching Gates and what he does and how he does it, and that's really

exciting in a behavioural way," says Jacqueline Novogratz, the founder and CEO of Acumen Fund, a non-profit global venture fund that uses entrepreneurial approaches to solve the problems of global poverty. *"It opens up people's minds to what's possible with philanthropy today."*[12]

When one sees him speaking one can feel that he is, or looks to be, very much at peace with himself relative to even the person he was 25 years ago. And the response of society to him is today far more positive in general than it was back then.

Warren Buffett

Warren Buffett[13] is a great example of somebody focusing early on his material account but who nevertheless never sacrificed any of his other accounts. Buffett was married to the same person for most of his life, and described it as incredibly happy, if somewhat unorthodox, relationship. Even though they separated decades ago they stayed best friends until her death and she actually introduced him to his second wife. He has, like Bill Gates, given away a very large part of his wealth to worthy causes. Buffett announced in 2006 that he would give away nearly $37 billion of his $44 billion fortune. The biggest share of this, almost $31 billion, was donated to the Bill & Melinda Gates Foundation, making it the largest charitable donation in history.[14] His statements reflect his belief that giving money to good causes is a way to create happiness for himself.

The respect that he has in the world because of that sense of integrity and decency in many ways confirms that looking after his emotional account in this way has been highly beneficial for him. Two of his most famous sayings are:

"It takes 20 years to build a reputation and five minutes to ruin it. If you think about that, you'll do things differently."

"It's better to hang out with people better than you. Pick out associates whose behaviour is better than yours and you'll drift in that direction."

Again here is a person who, well into his 70's, seems to be in excellent health, so somebody who has looked after himself very well physically all his life.

Oprah Winfrey

Success in the emotional account is not only much more difficult to gauge, it is also more difficult to point to as an obvious drive to outperformance than the other accounts. Having initially focused on her mental account to win a full scholarship to university, Oprah Winfrey achieved success early on in her career as a news anchor, but found her calling in Talk Shows through which she became a millionaire by her early thirties.

Her special talent has been her ability to create group catharsis without exploiting any individuals, and using empathy (she suffered a great deal in her early childhood, though she didn't make this public until an episode focused on sexual abuse in 1986) to create an environment of safety around those who have suffered. As Time magazine wrote in 2001:

"Few people would have bet on Oprah Winfrey's swift rise to host of the most popular talk show on TV. In a field dominated by white males, she is a black female of ample bulk... What she lacks in journalistic toughness, she makes up for in plainspoken curiosity, robust humor and, above all empathy. Guests with sad stories to tell are apt to rouse a tear in Oprah's eye... They, in turn, often find themselves revealing things they would not imagine telling anyone, much less a national TV audience. It is the talk show as a group therapy session."

She leveraged this ability through her philanthropic efforts, with Oprah's Angel Network in 1998, and setting up her Leadership Academy for Girls in South Africa six years later. Her famous on-air book club continued her efforts for her own and her viewers' mental accounts and in 1999 she received the National Book Foundation's 50th anniversary gold medal for her service to books and authors. She has also been a trail blazer in creating awareness of dietary issues in America using her empathy to encourage her audience to try, with her, various tactics to improve the physical account and could certainly no longer be described as being 'of ample bulk'.

Arnold Schwarzenegger

Arnold Schwarzenegger started out totally focused on his physical account:

"Arnold ... was often ill as a child. His ears stuck and he wore thick glasses. Shy and anxious ... at school Arnold was an average student..."[15]

From those beginnings Arnold Schwarzenegger built himself up to be the most famous and successful body builder of all time, winning the coveted Mr. Universe and Mr. Olympia titles many times. However he also looked after all his other accounts. After winning the majority of his body building awards he went back to studying and completed a degree in business and economics. He then built a successful acting career and became a multi-millionaire. Currently on his third career track, he is now widely respected as an environmentally-conscious governor of California. In addition, Arnold Schwarzenegger married into the most influential American dynasty, the Kennedys.

Please note that we took these 'extreme' examples to illustrate, not prove, our point. What is hard to dispute is that there are very few people in the world who enjoy universal respect and are seen as role models while having a large deficiency in any one of their accounts.

1.5   How are we going to use the Four Accounts?

We define success and long term sustainable happiness[16] as being one and the same. If you are not happy you have not achieved success but rather a trade-off between different accounts. Any trade-off leads to a cost and that cost will subtract from your total happiness, either immediately or later on in your life.

The next step is defining a gauge by which to measure success. The Four Accounts create clarity and specificity in what is being evaluated. All our plans going forward must therefore lead to measurable improvements in these four areas, in order for us to say that success has occurred. Success is equivalently defined as an **increase** in all Four Accounts. Excellence is then equivalent to **outperformance** in all the Four Accounts.

We want to emphasise this point: under this philosophy, outperformance in one to the detriment of another account is not considered success. In many cases, professional success and material wealth comes from sacrificing one's emotional and physical accounts over many years. This is trading between one's accounts, not succeeding.

The Four Accounts are closely interdependent, and can interact in both positive and negative spirals.[17] This interdependency is examined later in the book when we show how the outperformer can exploit it for his benefit through the creation of a virtuous cycle leading to an accelerating trajectory of success.[18]

1.6   How do the Four Accounts accommodate different people and dreams?

The desirable end amount and distribution of one's 'health and wealth' between the Four Accounts is unique to each person. What is important is that there is a sense of overall balance and that none of the Four Accounts is left neglected.

Some of the accounts will naturally outperform others in the medium and long term. **However, there will never be a point**

where you end up materially worse off, mentally less well or physically sicker as a consequence of following the strategies we outline. What may happen is that your physical health may not improve as quickly as your mental, emotional or material account, or vice versa.

However not only will there be a net positive for the Four Accounts overall, there will be a net positive for each and every account from the baseline. That is one of the key demands of this work, that there is no net loss in any of the accounts as you implement these ideas. To be perfectly clear – ageing impacts our physical account, but we are referring to any unnatural loss in the accounts here.

Each chapter after this – whether on love, vision, responsibility, networking, time management or study skills – is going to be focused on bringing about a very measurable increase in these Four Accounts, thereby moving you closer to success.

Key Takeaways: The Four Accounts

- There are four separate areas of a human being's personal assets that allow him or her to function in today's society. We call them the Four Accounts: emotional, material, mental, physical.

- The Four Accounts need a basic level of positivity in order for you to survive, and then a greater level of positivity in order for you to be happy.

- Success and long-term happiness are one and the same. They are defined as an increase in the Four Accounts, and this is the definition that is used going forward.

Don't forget the basics

- This book has two objectives. Firstly, to help you understand yourself and build solid foundations for your personal development. Secondly, to explain to you how to make use of the 80/20 principle and focus on 'picking the low hanging fruit'.

- The two principles are powerful on their own, but it is only when you combine them that you can reap the full benefits. Read both theory and practice with this in mind – they each contribute in a different way towards a common goal.

Chapter 2
Inspiration

"Really great people make you feel that you, too, can become great."

Mark Twain, author and humorist

"Whatever you can do, or dream you can, begin it. Boldness has genius, power, and magic in it."

Johann Wolfgang von Goethe, writer

2.1   How does our brain work?

The aim of this chapter is to discover the inspirational self-starter within us. To do this we need to know how our engine, the brain, really works and what has acted as its ignition, or motivator, in the past. Both inspiration and motivation carry very specific meanings in this book. Before we can define and differentiate between the two expressions, we need to make a little digression – in particular, we need to look briefly at the way the human brain is structured and how it operates.

There are four different parts[19] of the human brain, and they each contain a different intelligence:[20]

1. **The reptilian brain** is the most basic part of our brain. We make decisions about our survival here.

2. **The emotional brain** is the next part. It is here that we make sense of our feelings.

3. **The neocortex** is where our rational part resides, including reasoning ability and speech.

4. **The frontal lobe**[21] is the most advanced part of our brain. It contains advanced/spiritual intelligence[22] and its main purpose is to balance the other three intelligences in order to produce the best possible outcome for us as human beings.[23]

It is from the frontal lobe that ideas like increasing the Four Accounts in a balanced way, leading a balanced life, or going into philanthropy while pursuing material account gains in the same life originate.

2.2   What is Motivation?

Motivation can come from any of these brain parts and can take on many different forms. There is the motivation to survive that makes people do the remarkable when in danger, e.g.

in accidents, natural disasters or kidnappings. There is also fear-based[24] motivation; a lot of people fear getting fired from work and not being able to provide for their families.

In practice, fear has been used by 'mushroom managers' otherwise known as dictators and tyrants. The concept is simple: "Keep in a dark and cool place, cover in manure regularly". Fear and punishment compel obedience from one's employees. This recipe for replacing confidence with anxiety has proved popular because of the belief that underlings will only be vigilant and diligent through terror. Motivation can be based on other negative emotions, too – rage, cruelty, anger, jealousy. These are often thought to be a product of fear themselves and are all examples of motivation based on the reptilian and emotional brain.[25]

Mushroom management is the organisational method of choice for sweatshop owners. Sweatshops' practices, including forced overtime, low wages, and generally appalling working conditions, are the clearest example of exploitative intent. This is made possible by keeping the workers in the dark regarding their rights at work, and destroying their confidence through anxiety and stress. These are brought about by factory managers' punishments and fines for slow work, mistakes, and worker intimidation.

Sweatshops are becoming increasingly uneconomical for global companies especially in today's reputation-driven environment. In the past, short-term cost-cutting provided the rationale for outsourcing production to sweatshops. Public aversion to buying products resulting from such extreme mushroom management has however started to undermine the profitability of these practices.[26]

Employees in a high state of anxiety are likely to be less innovative and less productive in the long term. Furthermore, this strategy is harmful for the bosses – psychologists have shown that psychologically healthy people cannot be truly happy if they exert cruelty on others.[27] A number of global companies have consequently improved the conditions in their out-sourced operations, or abandoned the practice completely.

The success of Microsoft, Google, and the entire Silicon Valley culture, before, during, and after the dot.com boom has fortunately marked a shift to better motivation strategies. This happened first in the technology sector but has since spread to many other industries, and now there is a wide acceptance that there are better forms of motivation, especially inspiration.

2.3   What is Inspiration?

Inspiring people creates consistent outperformance. Inspiration can only come from the frontal lobe, the centre of our advanced intelligence.[28] Contrasting with motivation, inspiration is about seeing things with an open mind and working to discover what you love. It is a nurturing way of leading ourselves or someone else, a way to pursue our deepest desires and feelings, not to repress them.

Compare 'mushroom management' with the work environments created by companies committed to inspiring people: Google is the most famous example – the company's buildings are constructed to make the place feel fun, energetic and creative. The company not only allows, but actively encourages, their employees to spend 20%[29] of their time doing anything they feel passionate about, as long as it involves being creative and innovative. They care about the health and wellbeing of their employees and so frequently offer services such as gyms, massage rooms and medical centres on site. They also do small things like providing free food, drinks and snacks. In short, they make their people feel nurtured.[30]

On an individual level, an inspiring relationship is one where it is clear that your welfare is important to the inspirer, where you genuinely feel that the inspirer speaks to the part of you that responds to love. Hitler, for example, made many rousing speeches that moved people – but he incited them to hate. He was trying to connect with their prejudices and spoke to the most basic, reptilian and emotional, parts of the brains of the people who listened to him. An inspirer tries to connect with the loving part of one's brain. Gandhi and Martin Luther King were truly inspiring leaders as they constantly advocated forgiveness and non-violence. Equivalent principles apply to ideas, philosophies, or acts that inspire you.

> A person who inspires you accepts and supports you; he or she does not attack, judge or act in a malicious way towards you. Most importantly, he or she makes you believe in yourself.

There must be a real understanding by the person being inspired that the inspirer believes the ideas himself.

The honesty of the inspirer, and his ability to live up to what he advocates through his own behaviour, is crucial. His intent must be love and betterment of those he is trying to inspire; there must also be a sense of appreciation for the responsibility of his power to inspire. The opposite of this would be tobacco commercials[31] which made smoking sound like a cool life-affirming practice despite knowing that ultimately smoking would harm the smoker's health. Inspiration can only include things which the inspirer himself believes will lead to an increase in the Four Accounts of the audience. Have you ever noticed that a teacher who finds joy in his work is much more capable of creating enthusiasm in his or her students?[32]

This applies if the inspiration comes externally – inspiration can, however, also come from within. In this case, the part of us that is changing must feel that the part doing the cajoling also believes and really buys into the idea.

As a caveat, we should add that inspiration never leads to negative consequences in the medium and long term. Of course, there are trade-offs in the very short term. If you need to miss out on sleep in a reasonable way for a couple of days when meeting a deadline, this can be quite understandable as long as you compensate in a physically nurturing way afterwards. Such short term trade-offs are natural. In the medium and long term, however, inspirational ideas only lead to an increase in the Four Accounts.

Similarly, you are only truly inspiring yourself if you believe that the eventual target will help you and be right for you. If you believe that a certain activity is useless and you hate it, then motivating yourself to do well in it is not inspiring, even if you temporarily succeed in fooling yourself to think otherwise.

While you can be motivated to outperform in something that you do not like or even hate, you can never be inspired to it. If you try to inspire a tone deaf person to become a musician, he will most likely try very hard but find that he is just a much better mathematician. There will then come a point when inspiration mutates into some form of prodding as the person will stop being connected to his basic self.

2.4   Why is a loving intent fundamental to inspiration?

The human race has developed a very sophisticated – and actually quite remarkable – ability to fool ourselves, on an individual as well as a collective level. We convince ourselves that something is good for us when it obviously is not, or that something obviously bad is not as destructive as it seems. Most of us do this at least once a week – even if it is about small things such as food, entertainment, alcohol, guilty pleasures, procrastination and so on. Unfortunately, the same applies in politics, economics, business and international relations.

Many leaders of the past as well as those of today have used uplifting language for nefarious ends. The idea adopted by some fundamentalists, of many different religions, over millennia, that murder is permissible in the service of God(s), is completely perverse, as is any other agenda which involves the use of exalted ideas for an evil end. Using words in a way to bring about an end for which the words were not created is not inspirational, but manipulative.

Similarly, if we try to inspire ourselves but our underlying aims are not ones that would increase our accounts, then over time the same negative emotions – apathy, bitterness and so on – will take hold. We cannot lie to ourselves all the time – we can fool and trick our conscience for a while but eventually it will discover our falsehood.

> Lying to ourselves will never work in the long run because our conscience knows us and has access to the same underlying information about our intent as the part of the mind that is creating the manipulative language.

Inspiration can therefore only come from an intent that is honest, kind to ourselves, and is looking to benefit our accounts. Without that loving intent there will be a reaction, either in the short, medium or long term which will lead to a loss of energy and drive. This loss of energy and drive will then lead to failure. In the same way that if the foundations of a building are weak it will collapse regardless of its apparent integrity, if true inspiration is not behind our desires then somewhere on our journey of exerting ourselves as human beings we will fail to outperform.

This is why it is important that our inspiration really is inspiration, that it truly makes us feel energetic and enthusiastic. It also explains why we need a yardstick like enthusiasm to tell what truly inspires us.

2.5 What is enthusiasm and why is it important?

Most people today do not make a clear distinction between excitement and enthusiasm, so let's do that now. Enthusiasm is the almost constant, consistent state of optimism and happiness about your goal, and enjoyment during the journey to it. Enthusiasm can only come from within. Excitement, on the other hand, can be created both internally and externally. Excitement tends to be of much stronger intensity and often comes in short bursts that die away quickly.

Enthusiasm can be used as the ultimate yardstick for measuring if you are truly being inspiring to yourself or others. You know what genuine enthusiasm feels like and others can feel it too. This can help you recognise if you are inspired by something or if you have just found a clever new technique to manipulate yourself.

So actually, genuine enthusiasm tells you that you are on the right track and this is why it is so useful. As with any yardstick that is beneficial and effective, it makes sense to use it uniformly and consistently. But in order to do so you must be able to make the distinction between genuine enthusiasm and mere excitement.

2.6 How do we differentiate between enthusiasm and excitement?

Now that they are clearly defined, it should be relatively easy to distinguish between excitement and enthusiasm.[33] Excitement is often something that we have for a little while and then lose – whether it is physical excitement of any kind, including sexual, emotional or even mental excitement. Enthusiasm, on the other hand, is a long term consistent sense of wellbeing and is supported by a feeling of rightness about the plan, the idea, the mission, the journey, or the agenda. That is what differentiates it from excitement, and why it is so much more beneficial.

Enthusiasm is constantly uplifting and energy-providing. By contrast, excitement exhausts you eventually. Again, we can relate this to our description of how the human brain works. Excitement tends to come from the basic reptilian and emotional parts of our brain. Enthusiasm, on the other hand, can only come from a connection to the frontal lobe because that is where that sense of rightness within one's life really resides. Enthusiasm comes from emotional stability rather than emotional instability; it is entirely rational.

Inspiration creates enthusiasm. Enthusiasm is then the fuel of success. It is a specific emotion which creates that consistent, self-perpetuating energy that drives us forward. There is no sense within enthusiasm of needing a 'carrot and stick' approach; it is entirely a carrot approach. In fear-based motivation, while there is an adrenaline jump to create the action, there is still a concept of 'carrot and stick' with the stick being the negative consequence of not doing something while the carrot is actually the lack of punishment.

With enthusiasm it is easier to create and sustain a long-term commitment to something. Credibility and consistency come from enthusiasm. People who are genuinely enthusiastic about an idea, a venture, a job or anything else tend to be trusted implicitly. Enthusiasm has enormous power in winning you backers for your business, research project or anything else you may choose to undertake.

2.7   Virtuous cycles vs. Vicious circles

We have already mentioned the close interdependency between the Four Accounts. For the outperformer, it is this interdependency that allows him to create a virtuous cycle of consistent, constant improvements in his Four Accounts. For the underperformer, the opposite happens and a vicious circle of depression follows.

The depression circle is the belief that nothing you do will improve things, so you do nothing. More broadly, the depression circle can be used to describe many personal tragedies where underperformance in one of the Four Accounts leads to underperformance in others, making the initial problem even worse.

Some people get depressed about their appearance (physical account) and consequently start underperforming in relationships (emotional) and/or studies (mental). Others fall into financial trouble (material) which forces them to eat poorly and do less exercise (physical), as well as spend more time at work and less with friends (emotional).

These are generic examples – it is highly likely that you would have seen many specific ones in your own life or the lives of those around you. What your observations illustrate is that the depression circle is very real, and very common. A virtuous inspiration cycle is the complete opposite and is what real outperformers use to achieve excellence. Examples include:

- Michael Phelps, the record-breaking Olympic swimming champion. His enthusiasm for his goal of swimming excellence has led to a very healthy body (physical) and huge financial rewards (material). The reason we know that he has enthusiasm for his goal is the consistent dietary and exercise regime he has followed for many years and continues to follow even though there is no longer any survival pressure on him. Even though he suffers from attention deficit hyperactivity disorder (ADHD) he is able to stay totally focused on swimming.

  "One of the things I call Michael is the motivation machine. Bad moods, good moods, he channels everything for gain. He's motivated by success, he loves to swim fast and when he does that he goes back and trains better … anything

that comes along he turns into a reason to train harder, swim better. Channelling his energy is one of his greatest attributes." says his coach, Bob Bowman.[34]

Phelps is not perfect and has made his share of mistakes (brushes with the law, some experimentation with drugs). However he has recognised and apologised for these and continues to inspire himself and others.

- Tiger Woods is another inspirational athlete[35] as the first black man to win the US Masters golf tournament. Despite some setbacks he continues to bounce back onto the road to excellence. His enthusiasm for golf obviously continues undimmed even after he has accumulated substantial wealth and could easily have retired many years ago. He has also balanced family life with athletic achievements.

"Tiger trait number two is 'Create a clear and compelling dream ... what do you want to do with your life, and how will you get there?' ... Tiger Woods has a very simple and compelling dream", Booth says. *"He wants to be the greatest golfer of all time and to positively affect millions of lives."*

Woods has successfully channelled this dream to outperform.[36]

2.8   The benefits of empowered inspiration

Inspiration is not something of which we are the passive recipient, but rather something that we can proactively invite. The transition from being motivated by others, or the environment around us, to inspiring ourselves to success is beneficial not only for the tangible rewards but for the intrinsic increase in personal self-esteem that it delivers. The enthusiasm that comes from becoming a self-starter provides a measurable increase to our emotional account. When you are more confident you make better decisions about exercise, career etc. We will return to this topic later in a practical chapter on habits that help to develop and nurture inspiration.

One thing that hampers inspiration is that we tend, as humans, to use any yardstick until it becomes too painful to use, and then just change to a different one. Given that enthusiasm really works as a yardstick, it needs to be used uniformly and consistently. It will then act as a perfect barometer of your progress. It is vision that gives you the desire to jump on this virtuous cycle of consistent enthusiasm.

Key Takeaways: Inspiration

- The human brain has 4 parts – reptilian (survival), emotional (feelings), neocortex (rationality) and frontal lobe (advanced/spiritual intelligence).

- Motivation can originate in any part of your brain and can be fear-based. Inspiration, however, can only originate in the frontal lobe and is always based on an element of positivity.

- Enthusiasm is the best yardstick for inspiration. It is defined as the consistent state of positive and mild excitement about your goal, and about the journey to it.

- Virtuous cycles are situations where you leverage one account to increase another one and so on, leading to accelerating outperformance. Vicious circles are the opposite; they describe a situation when your problems in one account spread to the others.

Don't forget the previous chapter: The Four Accounts

- There are four separate areas of a human being's personal assets that allow him or her to function in today's society. We call them the Four Accounts: emotional, material, mental, physical.

- The Four Accounts need a basic level of positivity in order for you to survive, and then a greater level of positivity in order for you to be happy.

- Success and long-term happiness are one and the same. They are defined as an increase in the Four Accounts, and this is the definition that is used going forward.

Chapter 3
Vision

"The world makes way for the man who knows where he is going."

Ralph Waldo Emerson, philosopher and poet

"Your vision will become clear only when you look into your heart. Who looks outside, dreams. Who looks inside, awakens."

Carl Jung, founder of analytical psychology

3.1   What Are Objectives?

From the moment we come kicking and screaming into the world we have **primal needs**; we scream for food and warmth. A child knows that her need is being met through using her feelings, e.g. she feels better after her hunger is satisfied.

As we learn the language and become more aware of our surroundings, we start becoming influenced by desires that require the validation of others, our **interactive needs**. We start wanting to please our parents, be popular at school or excel in sports in order to get respect, recognition, or love. More specifically, our objectives may be to come first at our class, be on the football team and wear nice clothes so that other children think we are cool.

These are all objectives: academic, social, and emotional objectives. When they are met we feel better. That better feeling state is what drives us to create further objectives and work towards achieving them. As we mature, the very short term objectives become longer in duration and take longer to come to fruition. Whereas the objective of getting rid of hunger can be immediately achieved with food[37], the objective of being top of the class takes at the very least a homework assignment.

By the time we hit our teens, we start to think in terms of life objectives but the leap from objectives[38] to visions can take longer or may not happen at all.

3.2   What is Vision?

Vision, when realised, creates ongoing happiness. We define vision as a long-term goal which inspires you, creates enthusiasm and a sense of being able to make your mark in society.

Vision is driven by *inspiration*. This is what distinguishes it from objectives which come from *motivation*. Objectives, like motivation, can be fear-based. Surviving bullying, paying the rent, and not failing a class are all objectives. Vision, on the other hand, **always** comes from inspiration, and is characterised by **positivity**, **aspiration**, and a **long-term provision of happiness** if successfully implemented.

Consider, for example, ambitious academics and professionals who pursue their dreams without any regard for the rest of their Four Accounts. The difference between an objective and a vision is that the visionary realises he has to honour the Four Accounts during this journey. Importantly, he does so not in order to prevent burning out[39] from deteriorating health, but because he understands that the eventual goal is unlikely to bring him happiness without balance across his accounts.

Unfortunately, most people do not think about their 'life strategy' at all, or at best treat their life as a series of objectives. They therefore do not have a clear understanding of the long-term cost of achieving those objectives: sacrificing different accounts at different parts of their life. A true visionary would never make such sacrifices in the first place. She understands that even winning the Nobel Prize is unlikely to lead to long-term happiness if what follows is a life led without friends and in poor health.

When we follow a vision, rather than a series of objectives, we would never use harmful foods or drugs to deal with stress, or neglect friends to gain promotion at work. When truly inspired we seek to create a virtuous nurturing cycle between our four accounts rather than sacrificing one for the benefit of another. This is what guarantees long term happiness.

3.3   Why do most young people fail to follow a vision?

"Deferred gratification or delayed gratification is the ability to wait in order to obtain something that one wants. This ability is usually considered to be a personality trait which is important

for life success. It is an important component of emotional intelligence. People who lack this trait are said to need instant gratification."[40]

Most of us are to some degree biased in favour of instant gratification[41], as researched and documented by psychologists, behavioural economists and other scientists, this bias seems to be somehow natural to human beings. Successful adults tend to suffer from this bias to a lesser extent, mostly because they have some experience that allows their brain to fight this natural tendency.

The successful have, for example, already started earning high salaries and been able to afford nice things because they previously worked hard at university or in their job. This makes it emotionally easier to work hard again in order to get a promotion, compared to a student who is still at university and has not yet benefited materially from her hard work.

Conversely, the bias tends to be particularly acute for most young people and pretty much everyone suffers from it to some degree. In finance terminology, young people in particular tend to discount future happiness more than would be rational. If we assume that one chocolate today gives us the same pleasure as two in a year's time, it does not make sense to reject three chocolates in a year's time in order to get one today. But because of this well-documented bias, most children would accept one chocolate today.

> *It cannot be overemphasised how important it is for any visionary to truly understand the importance of this ability and to learn how to use it for his or her maximum benefit. Jan's story is a testimony to this – he is probably the most gifted individual I have met when it comes to his intuitive ability to internalise now the likely joy from the validation over the entire time spectrum. He just intuitively bases his choices on the entire utility curve across*

> time and therefore creates within himself enthusiasm for longer term objectives from very early on. The results speak for themselves and illustrate the value of learning this skill for others.

> Muzaffar

Earlier in life there is a tendency to be unaware of this bias, or a lack of desire to act on this awareness. This behavioural bias demonstrates itself through poor decision making in the present. For most people this is one of most common causes of underperformance relative to their potential. This is why we tend to follow objectives rather than visions, or at least be irrationally biased towards the former.

The bias drives you to join your friends for a pizza, latte or beer, followed by a DVD night, going out or playing football on the night before an important exam. Your brain knows that the exam is more important, but it also knows that even if you perform well, the payoff is going to come a long time ahead, when you perhaps get into a better university, or find a better job. On the other hand, your payoff from changing plans tonight is going to come immediately. So you put aside the books and head out.

A good illustration of this bias is Walter Mischel's 'Marshmallow Experiment' performed at Stanford University in the 1960s. A group of four-year olds were given a marshmallow and promised another, on the condition that they waited 20 minutes before eating the first one. Some children could wait and others could not. The researchers then followed the progress of each child into adolescence, and, using surveys of their parents and teachers, demonstrated that those with the ability to wait were better adjusted and more dependable, and scored an average of 210 points higher on the SAT (Scholastic Aptitude Test).[42]

In order for anyone to follow a vision, it is imperative that she has the ability to derive pleasure from future validation and success. The bad news is that very few people discover this ability by themselves. The good news is that it can be deconstructed and taught in easy-to-follow steps.

> Lying to ourselves will never work in the long run because our conscience knows us and has access to the same underlying information about our intent as the part of the mind that is creating the manipulative language.

3.4   How is the bias countered conventionally?

There are many people who earn a wage who work with passion and enjoyment but when an individual is too focused on objectives, at the expense of vision, they become subject to 'wage slave thinking'. These people do their job, up to a point, but cannot progress to become a true outperformer. A 'wage slave' will do only what they are told and not look to bring any creativity or inspiration to their workplace. They only do the work for which they know they will get instant gratification (wages, or a pass) and nothing more.

It is difficult to overcome this short time horizon bias, but employers, teachers and parents have found ways to minimise the 'wage slave' mentality. The simplest but least effective ones rely on resorting to 'discipline' (which becomes code for intimidation or punishment) as a way to try to focus the (young) person on a task whose positive emotional payoff is well in the future. As analysed in the earlier section on inspiration, punishment-based motivation cannot create long term enthusiasm. This results in studying being seen as a chore rather than as something to be enjoyed by most young people.

There are better ways; arguably the biggest difference between successful and underperforming schools is the way in which they address the bias towards instant gratification and the wage slave mentality that follows. The key to the success of many elite educational institutions is their ability to create the right set of incentives.

To start with, they have systems of creating peer pressure[43] which acts as a carrot and stick, depending on whether you are on track to achieve your (or arguably your parents') long-term goals. There is a collective sense of disappointment in you by those you look up to – teachers, parents etc. – if you underperform at the end of the year. Further, within your social group, there would often be a sense of not being as good as everyone else. This sense of a social punishment acts as a corrective for our short-term bias.

Another tactic is encouraging parents and teachers to work together to create material reward for long-term goal achievements. Parents following the punishment-reward strategy tend to give children gifts for academic achievement from a very early age, understanding the value of such achievement for their future success. At the extreme, we have seen cases where a student was given a Ferrari for getting his First class degree and securing a job at a top City firm. At the other end the reward can be a much simpler act of love like taking the child for his favourite day out (e.g. sports matches, movies etc.) or making him a special cake/his favourite food, linking both explicitly to his achievement.

This connection of immediate rewards for achieving goals with long-term payoffs acts as another balancer within the mind. Both the social respect and the judicious use of rewards act as Pavlovian[44] behavioural tools to change one's current behaviour in order to improve future outcomes. The idea behind both positive reinforcements is to create consequences now for failing to achieve or achieving goals with payoffs in the future.

> Simply explained, Pavlovian route refers to a well-known technique used to associate stimuli with events. If your parents, for example, always give you a present you really want in return for good grades, you will start associating good exam performance with pleasure that resulted from the presents you receive.

Clearly, this system does not work for everyone – some students still get expelled from even the very best schools. Nevertheless, it has been shown to be one of the more effective ways of correcting for the instant gratification bias. Outperformers, however, use a much more powerful tool.

3.5   Outperformer strategy

In most cases, it does make sense to use material rewards and punishments at the beginning of one's academic or professional career. But there comes a point in the life of most outperformers when carrot and stick does not work anymore: if you are truly good, you can escape most sticks and have enough carrots well before the end of your career. Those who continue to outperform tend to either love what they do, like Warren Buffet (one of the best investors in the world), or pay the price in their other accounts, like Michael Jackson (who has talked movingly about the emotional damage that the punishment/reward strategy of his father inflicted).

There are two fundamental risks with a punishment/reward strategy. Firstly, if you become too used to punishment, you can easily get so discouraged that at some point you decide that you just do not like competing. Secondly, what happens if the reward becomes sufficiently big for you to just grab it halfway through your journey, well before reaching your objective, and live off it for the rest of your life?[45]

If the carrot becomes sufficiently big you could adjust your goal to where you are at that moment; retire early when you feel that you have won enough competitions or respect, become sufficiently famous, made enough money etc. But that is not outperformance. That is being happy with what life has given you.

For the true visionary, the sense of that complete goal achievement feels really good and is not restricted to his material account. Whatever the field she is in, there is a real sense that getting there and the steps leading to it will create happiness within oneself. As we described earlier, that is enthusiasm.

The outperformer has to go within and find an intrinsic source of drive to constantly perform rather than be at the mercy of external reward/punishment. This is the difference between the wage slaves and those who excel and outperform within their field.[46]

The outperformer manages to connect within herself to a place where there is a real sense of joy about her future, a real sense of being able to visualise the happiness that would happen if certain goals were achieved. The way you know when a true sense of joy and happiness has been visualised is that all the steps to achieving that vision also creates happiness within you. There is never a sense of resentment about having to stay in and study, the current cost of pursuing the future goal of a good degree and then a good job. You have made the transition from objectives to your vision when there is no resentment for current sacrifices; then you really know that you are pursuing a vision because enthusiasm has spread throughout your emotional intelligence.

Consistency in positivity and mild elation makes the outperformers. They are different from those who are excited for a while but lose interest when that excitement dies out as well as those who are overwhelmed by the whole thing from the start. From an emotional intelligence point of view, consistency is the key. Once we have our emotional sense righted in this way and we feel an enthusiasm towards a goal, and throughout the journey to that goal, we can truly be said to have found our vision.

Real vision generates enthusiasm today towards your ideas for your future, creating happiness right now.

Key Takeaways: Vision

- You have objectives from very early on; they drive the majority of your actions, e.g. the need and desire to eat, sleep, relax, succeed at university and so on. Objectives come from motivation.

- Vision, on the other hand, is a long-term goal which inspires you, creates enthusiasm and a sense of being able to outline your place in society – in other words something that creates ongoing happiness.

- Delayed gratification – the ability to wait in order to obtain something that you want and to factor this in your decision making – is what distinguishes outperformers from others. It is at the very core of outperformance.

Don't forget the previous chapter: Inspiration

- The human brain has 4 parts – reptilian (survival), emotional (feelings), neocortex (rationality) and frontal lobe (advanced/spiritual intelligence).

- Motivation can originate in any part of your brain and can be fear-based. Inspiration, however, can only originate in the frontal lobe and is always based on an element of positivity.

- Enthusiasm is the best yardstick for inspiration. It is defined as the consistent state of positive and mild excitement about your goal, and about the journey to it.

- Virtuous cycles are situations where you leverage one account to increase another one and so on, leading to accelerating outperformance. Vicious circles are the opposite; they describe a situation when your problems in one account spread to the others.

Chapter 4
Love

"Love is the biggest eraser there is. Love erases even the deepest imprinting because love goes deeper then anything. If your childhood imprinting was very strong, and you keep saying: 'It's their fault. I can't change', you stay stuck."

Louise Hay, author

"Being deeply loved by someone gives you strength, while loving someone deeply gives you courage."

Lao Tzu, philosopher

4.1   Why do we need to redefine love?

Love, arguably the most important and frequently used concept in the world, does not have a widely accepted, universal
definition. If you ask the nearest three people for their definition of love, you are almost guaranteed to get three different
answers.

Whatever your definition, love tends to drive a significant
part of your actions and shape a large part of your life. This
is particularly true for young people who often struggle with
understanding themselves and their relationships. Detrimental relationships, whether with yourself or others, are then one
of the most important causes of underperformance at this age.
But why, if love is so central to us, has it picked up such a bad
press?

It is a reflection on the state of our culture that 'self-love' as
an expression has such a negative connotation; it sits closer as
a synonym to narcissism than self-esteem. As a result of this,
some psychologists continue to refer to self esteem rather than
self love, although this is a much narrower and less powerful
concept. In literature, or arts in general, love is often tragic,
and leads to the destruction of the lovers – *Romeo and Juliet*
is the quintessential example here. Poets highlight the pining
for the loved one to the exclusion of sleeping and eating. For
some psychologists, it is the idea of sacrificing your own wants
and wishes for the betterment of the other person that defines
love.[47]

Our culture therefore equates decreases in some of our four
accounts and unhappiness with the practice of love. The
reason why it is really important to change this perception
of love is that love tends to shape our basic system of beliefs
and values, as well as determining to a large degree what types
of relationships we are going to have. Correcting a sacrifice
based perspective of love by giving someone a definition that
is nurturing and supportive can have a massive impact on

their interactions in personal relationships and with society at large.

The entire focus of this chapter is to define love in a constructive way, and then discuss how practising this definition of love leads to excellence in your chosen field, and increased happiness in general. We want to show that far from being a vague idea, often with a negative impact on your life, love can actually be a clearly defined principle with specific practices that lead to tangible results.

4.2   How do we define love?

We want to dispose of this negative sentiment towards self-love as it is the fundamental building block of a healthy outperforming personality. It is a fallacy of today's world that one should build his personality only on love for others or mankind in general. The outperformer's sense of self-love and nurturing is what allows him to become a more loving person.

We define self-love as the intent to increase our own accounts in a kind, considerate and affectionate way. Humans are creatures of habits, full of rigidities, as we will discuss later. Self love is the best tool known to us that melts those rigidities.

Within our definition, a rationally loving person will not sacrifice themselves for the sake of the other but would rather find the course of action that would lead to the betterment of both individuals. This rationality, as the parameter within which love operates, is absolutely crucial to the outperformer: it means that love always leads to a net increase in the four accounts of both parties.

We define loving relationships as a consistent, rational interaction based on affection, consideration and kindness that create positivity in the Four Accounts of both parties.

It is important to note here that **this definition applies to all relationships** – friendships, romantic relationships, parent-child relationships, co-worker relationships and relationships with society at large.

Some of you may feel uneasy at first about 'demystifying' love in such a way, and taking away its 'magical' elements. Such fears are not justified when one gives this matter some further consideration. In fact, all our definition does is preserve the positive views of what is widely accepted as love while drawing a clear line between those and some of the undesirable, negative perspectives of love.

4.3   How to practise self-love

So how can love be practised towards oneself to create outperformance?

Discipline is the consistent performance of habitual tasks. What is often an implicit statement, when defining discipline, is that discipline is a consistent application of good habits. This is not strictly true. Alcoholics tend to be highly disciplined in that they habitually drink too much. Insomniacs tend to be disciplined in regularly forgoing enough sleep. Pessimists are quite disciplined in always seeing the worst in anything. It is not unusual to do things in a habitual way that are very damaging to ourselves, so a healthier perspective on discipline is required.

The difference between good discipline and bad discipline is the loving intention. Those who are self-loving follow habits that create in them a desire for, and then a faithful implementation of, good discipline. Those who are self-sabotaging in one form or another are really coming from an absence of self-love. Once you become truly aware of this one major difference between good and bad disciplines you can start to focus on, and see the rational reason for, self-love. The correction from bad to good discipline, therefore, is just self-love.

It becomes easier to practise self-love when you realise that it would drive you towards becoming healthier and physically fitter, more emotionally stable, mentally sharper and wealthier. When you truly believe in this conclusion then you can start to implement the good discipline habits and sustain them over your lifetime with ease.

The problem with good discipline is that many people see it as a form of self-sacrifice and a form of – it is not too much of an exaggeration – torture. Coming from that perspective, they create an unloving environment around their good habits.

In the morning they will set themselves really harsh sounding alarm clocks, jump into a stone cold shower to shock themselves awake and do all sorts of other things to shock and punish the body into doing something that they will believe is good for them. Once you realise that it is loving to have a good night's sleep – to go to bed early at night and wake up early in the morning as the body will respond best to that regime – then there will be more of a tendency to wake yourself with a gentler alarm clock.

Unloving actions for positive ends are self-defeating, in the long run, because they create resentment on the subconscious level. If it is understood that the action of waking yourself early in the morning is a loving act and nurturing to the body, then you can do a number of things to change this into a pleasant experience.

Set your radio, iPod or laptop to play your favourite music in the morning and give yourself 20 minutes to listen to that music, so that it will gently wake you up. Have your favourite food for breakfast, so that the body has something to look forward to on waking up. Add exercise in the mornings that you actually enjoy. Through food, music, enjoyable exercise or anything else that you enjoy, you can start sending your body some very loving messages. The body will then respond with less resistance to changing bad habits.

When you apply that idea into other areas of your life, you can see how good habits can slowly lead to an increase in your emotional account, making you happy.

You need to be careful while working on improving your life in this way though.

It is very difficult to make good rational decisions about changing negative things from a negative emotional state. It is therefore very important that you change your emotional state by focusing on the positive, and the loving intent is what allows this to happen. Then you can, from the positive emotional state, make rational decisions to change the negative aspects of your life.

4.4   Symbiosis

Problems arising from friendships and romantic relationships are some of the most important factors in young people underperforming relative to their potential. Developing the right perspective on what constitutes healthy relationships and creating an expectation of being only in healthy relationships are therefore two of the most important habits for the outperformer.

Healthy relationships are based on a consistent, rational interaction that leads to a **net** increase in the Four Accounts. This can allow for an **asymmetric increase in the emotional account of each individual** because happiness will ensue for both. Unhealthy relationships, on the other hand, are characterized by making us feel bad about ourselves, causing us to make decisions out of loyalty rather than personal integrity, tempting us to gossip about other people rather than discussing ideas.

Symbiosis is a great way of thinking about relationships and networks in general. What is often misunderstood is that symbiosis does not mean living peacefully next to each other – that is harmony, or liberty, not symbiosis. Symbiosis means that both parties must actively get something from the interaction, they must both be nurtured.[48]

Consider teaching – what happens between the two individuals is that the teacher is giving his time to impart knowledge, i.e. increase the mental account of the student, and, within the western society parameters he is being paid for it, so his material account is increased. In this case, the accounts of both individuals are increased in the interaction.

What is less obvious is the productivity gain that occurs when he teaches lovingly, i.e. from the intent of consideration, kindness and affection. The teacher creates gentleness in communication that produces an effect on the student of feeling a loving gratitude, thereby making him more open to learning. This positive emotional response in the student leads to a greater ability to absorb knowledge. Mutual nurturing is the key to healthy relationships.

4.5   Reciprocity

The way that we can tell if we are in loving relationships is to see how many of our relationships cause us to feel weary and needy, and how many make us feel free, inspired and loved in a nurturing way. The crucial insight of the outperformer is to realise that needy and fearful relationships have opportunity cost in terms of the mental, emotional, physical and material drain they produce. Once this is understood the recognition of the importance of, and desire for, loving relationships follows. That insight can, in turn, produce more incentive in you to follow out the intent of your inspired self. Looking at the opportunity cost of fooling yourself that you have achieved things that you have not, you can see what it would have been like if you had been truthful to yourself.

The more there is a sense of clarity about what is under your control, the more you will stop wasting time on things over which you have no control at all. One of the greatest emotional mistakes that a lot of people make is to waste time on trying to make other people like them[49], and we are talking primarily about romantic relationships here. The outperformer realises – and this is a form of emotional maturity – that there are certain people with whom he has a natural connection and that there are others with whom he does not; even more importantly, he realises that this does not in any way say anything about his general lovability.

However most people wrongly take responsibility for how other people feel about them. They try to make other people like them regardless of how this makes them feel. It is very important for the outperformer to realise that if the same consistent love that one is giving is not being reciprocated, then the relationship is not symbiotic in a healthy way. One must then find ways to decrease one's interaction with that person over time because while it is possible to change others if one gives enough kindness, consideration and affection consistently over a long enough period of time, the opportunity cost of doing so is too high for the outperformer in most cases.

If you spend most of your time loving those who return that sentiment you will find that you can have ten loving relationships over the same period that it would take you to convert one unloving relationship into a loving one. This opportunity cost is what makes the outperformer realise that responsibility is mutual and that the other person must be held accountable for their part in the relationship as well.

Once this is truly understood and accepted, a huge amount of time can be saved. Trying to make someone who does not love you change his or her mind is one of the most prevalent ways of wasting time in people's teenage years and actually well into their twenties. And there is a very real cost to such behaviour:

- It wastes your **emotional account**, because you could be in ten other mutually loving relationships feeling good about yourself, rather than feeling miserable.
- It wastes your **material account**, because that is a time when you could be out making money, doing more study to gain better qualifications, or coming up with inspiring ideas.
- It wastes your **mental account** because you could be in loving relationships with inspiring people, who generate new positive avenues of thought for you to focus on, rather than thinking "Why does this person not like me?"
- Finally, such behaviour wastes your **physical account** because rejection in love leads many to loss of appetite, excess thereof and/or abuse of alcohol and other harmful substances as a way of coping.

Not holding the other person responsible in a mutual relationship is a large net negative in every possible way. This is the reason why it is so important to only engage in romantic relationships with those who would love us back in the same way.

This rule is equally important for our networks, colleagues and in every other relationship. Work for bosses who are nurturing, kind, affectionate and leave jobs where the managers are continuously looking to create a toxic environment. Join communities – online or offline, neighbourhoods etc. – which act with the same love towards you that you give to that community.

If your networks are made up of 'toxic' people then they will be a drain on you but if your networks are mutually nurturing then they will become very beneficial in your life. The difference between the two is easy to spot by the way you feel. If you feel energised, enthusiastic and happy about yourself then you are in a nurturing network. If you feel bad about yourself, if you start doubting yourself or feel physically exhausted, then you know that you are in a draining network.

Understanding that you have no one to fear, regardless of your and their position, and that no one has the right to treat you badly lies at the very basis of healthy relationships. Indeed, when we start a relationship or join a network with low self-esteem, we tend to become a little obsessive and end up in a position where we are more likely to sacrifice something for that network or relationship.

What is interesting is that networks and relationships tend to mirror the kind of behaviour we exhibit. It is therefore important to take responsibility for the fact that you should be feeling happy, as this is a part of your agreed relationship with yourself. When joining networks or starting relationships one must expect and demand to be treated well and with respect. In most cases one will then be indeed treated in this way.

4.6 Love and philanthropy

You may have been thinking "hang on, they said we don't suffer in our material account, but does that mean we can't give to charity?"

Firstly, a disambiguation: within this perspective you could still work for a charity or non governmental organisation if your intent was to make a career in this field. Your mental account would be increased because you would be learning on the job and also you would be getting paid as an employee. In choosing which charity to work for, apply the same criteria of having inspiring managers who encourage loving relationships within the organisation. That way, when it is your time to lead in the charity field, you are spreading good management practices as well as contributing through the charitable mission.

But what about giving money away to charity? Is that wrong?

We said at the very beginning that our strategies and principles would never lead to a net decrease in any of the Four Accounts. We then defined love consistently with this, as an interaction that leads to a net increase in each of the individual accounts. **But then, how does one classify philanthropy, often perceived as the ultimate act of love?**

Man is a herd animal. Freud said that after their basic primal needs are satisfied, man craves recognition by his fellow man.[50] This is proven by the joy we feel when we receive prizes or compliments. The key to accessing this joy in a loving manner is to contribute positively to society without any decreases in our four accounts. Going into politics or joining charities as long term careers fulfils these criteria. You get paid more as you progress in those careers, increase the number of loving relationships you have with people and do not have any negative connotations for the mental and physical accounts. But it is important at this stage in your life that you follow these arenas as careers, which causes no decrease in your accounts, and not in a philanthropic manner for reasons discussed below.

Within our parameters, we could not classify Bill Gates' decision to establish his foundation and give away $30 billion as love[51]. Clearly, for him to have made this decision, it must be the case that the reduction in his material account has to be compensated by whatever increase he gets in his emotional and mental accounts.

We would still want to define this as love, but then we would have to define love as an act where there is a net positive benefit overall as opposed to a net positive benefit in each of the four accounts individually. However we said that there must never be a net decrease in any of the Four Accounts in the medium and long term.

When you go to university and pay for it, both in fees and living expenses, as well as foregone earnings, this still works under our definitions. The reason is that there is a monetary value in the asset – university degree – that you obtain. Your material account has not gone down – you just changed one form of wealth (cash) into another (skills). With charity it is a bit more difficult.

This is why we put a provision into our definition of love, and defined it in such a way for our target audience – young people. The natural human cycle of saving and spending explains why this makes sense. The period of a child's life should be and is normally one of unconditional receiving – between birth and age of at least 16 you tend to be a net taker of everything without any real trade-off happening. The converse is true in the period of old age when human beings tend to be natural spenders. So within those areas different rules tend to apply.

This makes perfect sense. After all, when you are on an aeroplane and the oxygen masks come down, you are much better off putting on your own oxygen mask first and then helping others, rather than the other way round. In order to help others, you need to be in a position to do so – this corresponds to having high balances in all of your accounts. For the outperformer, early years are definitely a time of looking after themselves in order to be able to look after society later on in life if that brings them happiness.

Becoming too philanthropic with your accounts at too early a stage can actually reduce your impact in the world later because you are not cumulatively building up assets and you are not building up wealth for yourself. This is why for the age group to which this book is directed, loving interactions within this period should always lead to an increase in the Four Accounts and never at the expense of another account in the medium and long term. Where we have talked about education and paying for it – that is an investment, not expenditure.

You need to be financially secure, mentally agile, emotionally happy and physically fit, and to have valuable skills and experience before turning your attention to philanthropy. It is then with those securities that you can then lead a different life in your 30s and beyond. The earlier period however must be about self-investment in the Four Accounts for the outperformer so that a self-perpetuating success cycle is created.

4.7   Reflection and self analysis

We have tackled some difficult and highly personal issues in this chapter and it is only natural that you should now start to think through how this explanation of love applies to you. However, self-evaluation should also be done with a very clear idea that it must not become obsessive self-analysis. What often happens, in those who are looking to outperform, is that if they do it all by themselves they can end up being too obsessed with perfection and so spend far too much of each day, month or year looking at all the negatives. You must understand very clearly that it is important to have a list, and it is important to work through it, but there should be a very strictly limited period of time allocated to this exercise.

The majority of your time should be spent on being grateful for and focused on that which is going right in your life. What you will find if you are honest with your self-evaluation is that **the majority of your life tends to work pretty well**. We actually do most things right and without a problem. Most of us tend to be able to get up, go to work, eat, sleep, breathe etc. and more than 90% of the functions we do in a day, we do perfectly.

Too much self-criticism can also be a path to depression and that must be avoided.[52] Healthy criticism is only healthy if the time allocated to it within the day, month or year is balanced. It is too easy for people to become paralysed by self-criticism. This is another way that love is very powerful. A self-loving person will be able to see that too much criticism is a form of self-attack; he will begin to feel bad if he attacks himself too much.

This is especially true for many of the things that cause you to become upset or discontent, but are truly outside of your control. Human beings have a tendency to focus more on things that make them feel bad rather than things that make them feel good. Many of us tend to be angry when we do not get a pay rise but not be equivalently happy when we have been receiving good pay. This sense of over-focusing on bad things can have, to some limited degree, a positive impact as it drives you to perfection and success but again balance is the key.

The same thing applies when you are taking an inventory of things that are not going well, and individuals that are not being pleasant, in your life. Once you have made an inventory, you must first change your emotional state to positivity about what is working. It is from this happier emotional state that you look for solutions to the problems. The better emotional state will beget far better solutions. The negative emotional state of feeling helpless or overwhelmed by your problems will actually lead to sub-optimal decisions.

Even with all the bad events and bad people acting towards you, for the majority of the people in the western world, most of your interactions during the day tend to be relatively courteous and positive. It is always important to have a perspective, and realise that actually most people are helpful to you and that the vast majority of things are going smoothly. That balanced perspective creates the emotional state from which rational decisions about the improvement of the negative things in your life can come.

Key Takeaways: Love

- Love drives a significant part of our actions but there is no consensus on its meaning.

- Love is defined as a consistent, rational interaction based on affection, consideration and kindness that creates positivity in the Four Accounts of both parties.

- Rationality, as the parameter within which love operates, is absolutely crucial to the outperformer. It is this area where love has so often been misunderstood.

- Love is the intent to increase others' accounts; self-love is the intent to increase our own accounts in a kind, considerate and affectionate way. Self-love is the fundamental building block of a healthy personality.

- The fundamental difference between bad discipline (alcoholics, insomniacs, bullies) and good discipline (positive habits) is the loving intent.

Don't forget the previous chapter: Vision

- You have objectives from very early on; they drive the majority of your actions, e.g. the need and desire to eat, sleep, relax, succeed at university and so on. Objectives come from motivation.

- Vision, on the other hand, is a long-term goal which inspires you, creates enthusiasm and a sense of being able to outline your place in society – in other words something that creates ongoing happiness.

- Delayed gratification – the ability to wait in order to obtain something that you want and to factor this in your decision making – is what distinguishes outperformers from others. It is at the very core of outperformance.

Chapter 5
Responsibility

"Freedom is the will to be responsible to ourselves."

Friedrich Nietzsche, philosopher

"I am free because I know that I alone am morally responsible for everything I do."

Robert A. Heinlein, novelist

5.1   Why do we need to redefine responsibility?

'Responsibility', like 'love' has a whole array of definitions depending on who you ask. Its use in common language reflects this confusion, which then further cascades into our collective misunderstanding of what we should actually feel responsible for, often confusing it with obligation.

The key difference between this book and the conventional wisdom is that we urge you to not focus on any feelings of guilt or other self attacking emotions that may arise as a result of your irresponsible acts. Rather, having honestly accepted that you have acted irresponsibly, immediately focus on getting back in touch with your inspirational thoughts and getting into the emotional state of feeling enthusiastic again. This will lead to new actions that will be highly beneficial to your Four Accounts and is the best redemption for past irresponsibility.

5.2   What is our definition?

We separate responsibility into two different cases and use the following definitions.

- When used in the context of being responsible **for** something, we define responsibility as having the power to control and change it.
- When used in the context of behaving responsibly **towards** something, we define responsibility as behaving in accordance with our intent.

For the outperformer the intent is always loving – to increase the Four Accounts to bring about long term success and happiness. **Loving intent underpins the outperformer's perspective on responsibility.**

To illustrate lets take the example of the environment: it is often stated that human beings are responsible for the environment and that we have responsibility towards the environment. Can you tell what exactly each of these statements mean? In particular, what is our responsibility towards the environment?

When we say human beings are responsible for the environment, an empowering way of looking at it is that we have the power to control and change the environment. Whenever we say that we have responsibility towards the environment, we must also specify our intent towards the environment. If our intent is to destroy the rain forests of this planet, then chopping down trees, in order to use the land for agriculture, would be perfectly responsible![53]

Expanding on our previous definition of responsibility in general, we define personal responsibility as the ability to control and change ourselves, or equivalently as a contract to act in accordance with our intent. Please note that we are separating ourselves (our intent) from our actions.

What this definition does is make it impossible to say that one is being irresponsible without first defining one's intent. How many times have you heard your parents say that you have behaved irresponsibly while you thought that your actions were perfectly responsible? The difference clearly lies in your and your parents' differing views on what should be the intent of your actions.

To illustrate this further – most people would classify constantly partying like an animal, running into a different scandal every week and getting arrested as seriously irresponsible behaviour. Do you agree?

What if your original *intention* is to party like an animal, run into a different scandal every week and get arrested? You may find this funny, but it is actually not as ridiculous as it sounds. Consider someone like Paris Hilton, who may well say "Look, I have an image. If I live up to that image, then there is a certain section of society that will approve of this behaviour and actually pay me for wild partying".

One of the reasons that Paris Hilton gets certain TV and film roles is that she is a famous personality that people will go and watch. The reason it is interesting to see her in the show *Simple Life* is that she is anything but simple. Her very way of living has become part of her brand. Her lifestyle is therefore actually very responsible.

Let us look at another example, say a Sergeant in the British Army or a Command Master Chief of the United States Navy Seals. Here it is perfectly possible that although they act in a manner that looks cruel or harsh their intent is to help soldiers survive in war, so they are being perfectly responsible in the context of what they are doing. The same kind of treatment that those instructors employ towards soldiers would be irresponsible towards a highly sensitive three year old child. **Intent and context are not separable from our actions when discussing responsibility.**

5.3   Why is our definition of responsibility more useful?

Most people's intent is to have a healthy, beautiful body even though they drink way too much alcohol, eat low nutritional content foods that are bad for them, sleep too much or too little, do no exercise, smoke etc. They are therefore behaving irresponsibly as their actions are in disagreement with their intent. But why do we act irresponsibly?

Many people see responsibility as a burden; we see it differently. **Responsibility is the understanding that you have the power to do something in a situation, about a situation, for an individual or to an individual. Responsibility at its core is actually the ability to respond.** Most people misunderstand this completely.

Most people think that if they are responsible for something, they should feel guilty if they do not use that power wisely, they should attack themselves if they fail, or feel bad about any failures in their area of responsibility, and they should be obliged to always act in a certain way. Any failure to live up to their responsibility then leads to a negative emotional spiral.[54] This in itself then leads most people to actually start avoiding responsibilities over time, as failure is emotionally too painful.

But the entire dynamic changes if you start using our definitions. **When you see responsibility as something within your power** rather than as something with which to criticise, that shift in focus can actually over time **create enthusiasm in you to act responsibly**. You start seeing it as a power within you to start acting responsibly.

5.4   What is responsible in the context of this book?

Seeing responsibility as a power rather than obligation lies at the very basis of this book. You do not *have* to think positive thoughts but you have *the power* to think such thoughts. You have the power to read this book and change your life for the better if better is defined as increase in the Four Accounts, but there is no obligation to do so.

You are changing your life all the time, whether intentionally or unintentionally, and the key to responsibility is to understand this fact. The greater the understanding of what lies within the domain of your responsibility, the greater your ability to choose which areas you want to focus on to exercise that power. The principles we outline should also help you understand that there are things for which you may feel responsible despite actually having no responsibility for them what-so-ever.

We have outlined a very specific loving intent in this book – to increase your Four Accounts. To behave responsibly therefore means for us to write in a way that increases your accounts. The ideas, action points and strategies of this book are therefore responsible given that intent. Analysing if you are behaving responsibly vis-à-vis your intent will produce a sense of accountability which will, over time, lead to a positive modification in your behaviour. It will also lead you to focus your inspiration, vision and love for the service of your intention. That laser like focus is what will lead you on to the inside track for success and happiness.

Those who act in this responsible manner towards others, as well as themselves, create a persona that subconsciously makes people trust them and want to interact with them. This combination of responsibility and love will ultimately lead to inspiration internally and charisma when dealing with others.[55] Needless to say, charisma has huge influence on your romantic relationships, your friendships, your business relationships and later on in life on your relationship with the society in large. Fortunately, it all starts from here, focusing on a lifetime of responsibility and love towards ourselves and others.

Key Takeaways: Responsibility

- Responsibility is used in many conflicting and confusing ways in today's society; we therefore provide a clear definition. When used in the context of being responsible for something, we define responsibility as having the power to control and change it. When used in the context of behaving responsibly towards something, we define responsibility as behaving in accordance with your intent.

- Personal responsibility is the ability to control and change yourself, or equivalently it is a contract to act in accordance with your intent. Note that we are separating your self (your intent) from your actions.

- Many people incorrectly see responsibility as a burden. In fact, responsibility is the understanding that you have the power to do something in a situation, about a situation, for an individual or to an individual.

- When you see responsibility as something within your power rather than as something with which to criticise, that shift in focus can actually over time create enthusiasm in you to act responsibly.

Don't forget the previous chapter: Love

- Love drives a significant part of our actions but there is no consensus on its meaning.

- Love is defined as a consistent, rational interaction based on affection, consideration and kindness that creates positivity in the Four Accounts of both parties.

- Rationality, as the parameter within which love operates, is absolutely crucial to the outperformer. It is this area where love has so often been misunderstood.

- Love is the intent to increase others' accounts; self-love is the intent to increase our own accounts in a kind, considerate and affectionate way. Self-love is the fundamental building block of a healthy personality.

- The fundamental difference between bad discipline (alcoholics, insomniacs, bullies) and good discipline (positive habits) is the loving intent.

Intermission

Responsibility concludes the theoretical part of this book, and we are now moving to the more practical chapters. As we do that, it is important for you to understand how the two interact, and why they are particularly powerful when implemented together.

Book One has explained why it makes sense to work on improving your Four Accounts, and how they lead to happiness and success. It has also addressed a number of potential dangers. Dealing with self-sabotaging instincts through focusing on inspiration, love and positive relationships is perhaps the most important of these lessons.

Theory provides the reasoning that underpins the need for change. It also gives you the tools to increase your chances of successfully implementing the strategies we are about to outline. The outperformer uses his left brain to generate enthusiasm first and inspire him- or herself to go and change whatever needs changing in his or her life. Giving yourself a logical explanation of the reason for change, and benefit thereof, will make it much easier to motivate yourself properly, and commit seriously to the decision.

Book Two completes the double-helix that constitutes the real core of our work. It creates a powerful virtuous cycle which inspires the practical implementation of ways to excel. In turn, the practical results of excelling provide both emotional and rational feedback that increases commitment. The theory and practice therefore mutually support and reinforce each other.

Practice is generally structured by the account that is dominant in a given chapter. Chapters 6–9 are broad and look at all the accounts. Chapter 10 works on increasing your physical account, chapters 11–13 look at your emotional account and finally Chapters 14–16 focus on the mental account. Chapter 17 brings everything together and explains why we do not talk in great detail about the material account. It looks at the broader impact of your leisure activities, and outlines why your material account is just a by-product of your lifestyle. The underlying idea is to change leisure from a time to vent and be self destructive to a period of relaxation that is also productive, i.e. increasing your Four Accounts.

Balance is a concept we use often, and it applies here too. For one, as most entrepreneurs will tell you – ideas are easy, execution is difficult. Equally, however, great execution without a sense of direction or meaning will get you nowhere. The theory we have presented in previous chapters forms solid foundations for your future development. The challenge now is to build your life on those foundations – or, equivalently, to execute on your vision.

Book Two
Practice

Chapter 6
Measurability and Yardsticks

"I do not try to dance better than anyone else. I only try to dance better than myself."

Mikhail Baryshnikov, dancer

"Don't measure yourself by what you have accomplished, but what you should have accomplished with your ability."

John Wooden, basketball coach

6.1   What and why do we need to measure?

Shortly we will be looking at the practical skills and habits that you need to develop to achieve your vision, but in order to determine their efficacy it is important to have external and stable benchmarks. If you think of yourself as a business, the Four Accounts are analogous to the balance sheet; our progress in increasing them corresponds to profit and loss account; our habits and processes are in many ways similar to the way the business operates.

There will be areas where you are already doing relatively well (your starting capital if you like) and others that need augmenting; there are therefore two things we need to measure and evaluate. Firstly, we need to measure the balance in our accounts[56], and the corresponding increases, and secondly, we need to evaluate those increases against external benchmarks to make sure that we are doing things in the best possible way, similarly to a business which would benchmark itself against its competitors.

6.2   How to measure the changes in accounts

Measuring is easier for some accounts than for others. Most of you will be very familiar with one of the most (un)popular ways of measuring increases in our mental accounts. They come towards the end of the academic year, and are something that schools and universities put us through in order to see if our brains are working – yes, we are talking about exams. More broadly, you can use many different types of tests, ranging from IQ tests to various qualifications, language tests etc. to see if your mental capacity is increasing. But the very best way to measure if your mental capacity is improving is actually to notice the number of interesting, out-of-the-box and/or inspiring thoughts you have on a daily basis.

Emotionally speaking, the best yardstick – and this is a tough one to honestly gauge – is how are our relationships coming along? Are we having relationships that are nurturing us and are we nurturing the other individual? How many of our relationships are nurturing and how many are parasitic in some way in nature? Are we perhaps even being self-destructive? This tends to be a better yardstick of emotional health than any other because there is someone else, some external person involved. It is very easy to temporarily fool ourselves along the "Ah, I'm happy" lines. Relationship monitoring tends to keep us honest in that if we have relationships which are mutually nurturing, then we know that we are making positive progress with our emotional account. We will look at relationships in more detail in a separate chapter later in the book.

Measuring our material account would seem relatively easy, but actually, the opposite is the case. The reason for this is that we are concerned not only with our bank account balance but with all of our assets. This includes tangible things, such as new equipment or tools, but also intangible assets which are – similarly to the problems faced by real businesses – much more difficult to value. The most obvious examples of intangible assets that many of you have or will acquire are education and professional qualifications. How do you place a monetary value on your degree?

Those of you who have done some accounting will know that there are several options. For example, one could take the 'net present value of probable incremental cash flows', where you value your degree as the discounted increase in the lifetime earnings you are likely to achieve because of having that degree. This is a sensible strategy – after all, most graduates from good universities in the world make at least as much extra income over their lifetime as the amount they lose not working the university years, even adjusting for inflation. The benefits of higher social status, contacts and broader personal development are a welcome extra benefit. Fortunately, there probably will not be too many large, intangible assets entering your calculations. And for those that are, making the conservative assumption that your material account does not change – i.e. cash down, qualifications up, summing to zero – should do the trick.

Last but not least, performance in sports or exercises you do regularly is a very good way of measuring increases in your physical account, particularly when coupled with considering your overall health. Relative to last week, are you running just as fast, lifting the same weights, swimming the same length, cycling as fast without losing breath? Choose something that is easily quantifiable and measurable, and see if your habits lead to consistent, significant increases in your performance.

6.3   Defining the specific yardsticks

There are two ways to improve a process: efficiency and leverage. Our definitions are as follows:

> **Efficiency** means improving the way we do things in order to achieve a given amount of output with minimum inputs, or conversely to achieve maximum output for a given set of inputs.

> **Leverage** means fundamentally changing the way we do things in order to achieve efficiency gains of 100% or more.

These are two very distinct ways in which you can improve a process – you can either do so in small, incremental steps of a few percentage points (efficiency), or you can just entirely change the nature of the game (leverage). A good historical example would be improving the system of sails on medieval ships versus the invention of steam engines and therefore the steam-wheeler ship.

The Fosbury Flop was another great example: a style used in the athletics event of high jump, it was revolutionary when first introduced because it reversed the position in which athletes cleared the bar and is now the only style used competitively, In both cases the innovation enhanced the activity radically. Leverage events happen rarely but yield dramatic improvements.[57]

Accordingly, we define efficiency as constant, gradual improvements in a process. Leverage is used to describe situations where we change the process in a fundamental way.

6.4   How to evaluate the way we increase our accounts

Why do we need to evaluate the way we increase our accounts? Let's go back a few chapters to where we defined responsibility as acting in accordance with our loving intent. In practice we need to "act in accordance with our loving intent *in the most efficient and leveraged way.*" Let's illustrate this with an example:

Consider a student who regularly campaigns for increased protection of the environment. Most people would see such a student as a role model, and a conscious, responsible citizen. We could not disagree more. In fact, there is a very limited benefit to a student leaving his university, whether for a few days to take part in some sort of political agitation, or for six months to camp in woods in order to protect them from being cut down.

There are, on the other hand, many ways to pursue the same ideals with much greater impact. He could go and study economics or environmental science and write about the opportunity cost of cutting down forests. He could join a government or non-government organisation involved in the relevant decision making process. Alternatively, the private sector has recently started to capitalise on the opportunities in protecting the environment in innovative and profitable ways; the student could join a corporation looking to harvest the wood sustainably. There is also the option of joining companies producing environmentally friendly products, e.g. electric cars, solar panels, wind turbines etc. – the list goes on.

Moreover, there is always the opportunity to simply outperform in any field and make enough money to pay for 100 other political activists to go and camp in the woods. The key point is that the outperformer shares these ideals but is looking to find a leveraged way to contribute to the goal.

There is a deep, fundamental difference between the conventional definition of responsibility and the outperformer's definition. Having understood one's loving intent, responsibility means achieving the most efficient and leveraged outcome, not just making a step in the right direction.

One of the best ways of monitoring if you are living up to the responsibility of creating leveraged results is by checking the opportunity cost of your actions. For example, people often see fees as the main cost of going to university. In fact, there is a much bigger cost involved – the opportunity cost of going to university consists of the earnings you could have earned if you went directly to work, as well as the fees you pay.

This is a very left brain analysis and solution. Some people, who are more right brain orientated, perform this function intuitively and are said to have high emotional intelligence. The way they know that they are acting responsibly is that they feel happy and they trust that feeling to guide them through life. Happiness in this context is a sense that a given decision feels right, that the decision feels beneficial.

6.5   How to create efficiency and leverage

Efficiency is very powerful in that it is a relatively predictable process that is usually easy to replicate across activities and accounts. Leverage is a more difficult beast: it comes from seemingly random, spontaneous ideas, though one can definitely develop the right mindset for generating and spotting leveraged opportunities.

The way that most efficiency gains come about is through learning from others by watching them, reading relevant articles and books and adopting best practices used by your friends and colleagues. There is also a contribution from constantly evaluating the way you do things, and trying to improve your processes for the better. In many ways, this is similar to the principle of Kaizen[58] – continuous improvement – which was popularised by Japanese corporations in the second half of the last century.

Measure efficiency per time unit – a day, an hour or other suitable period. This allows you to correct course very quickly rather than following ineffective regimes.

Learning certain skills and habits, outlined in the following chapters, will help create efficiency in your life. Once you have implemented this generic framework, you should start applying the Kaizen mindset described above as this will help you take this process many steps further.

Creating leverage is a much less structured process that is very difficult to describe or quantify. Leverage relates very closely to lateral thinking, as it often arises as a consequence of thinking outside the box and thereby doing things in unconventional ways or accessing unexpected resources. It has certainly been the case in our experience that the decisions which created the most leveraged results resulted directly from ignoring or breaking certain conventional wisdoms, universal truths or widely accepted principles.

Independent thought is often the key to leveraged results. The best way to develop a questioning, critical mindset that is at the same time capable of innovation and thinking outside the box is to always ask insightful questions, and build on the principles we describe in the chapter on lateral thinking.

Both of us understand and are committed to the importance of mentoring. Muzaffar has for several years mentored a number of highly successful people in fields ranging from international finance to textiles, and lately, some London School of Economics students. Jan has also been involved in various mentoring schemes over the last few years. We have both used a number of techniques to increase the efficiency of such activities, including better ways to organising meetings, following up, to-do lists, better specified goals, and so on.

Having seen the difference one can make to other people's lives by giving them the right advice, most mentors at some point start thinking about how to address a greater number of people. Putting our mentees into groups and organising joint meetings was one way of achieving this goal. It is also a very good example of leverage – not just because it saved time for us but because it allowed the mentees to share best practices and start helping each other too.

Recognising that even with group mentoring there was a limit on how much we could achieve, deciding to write this book is an even better example of what we mean by leverage – this is not about achieving some incremental improvements but about changing the game entirely. With this book we are now hoping to help millions of young people change their lives for the better; we couldn't dream of reaching and helping so many one to one or with group-based mentoring.

Key Takeaways: Measurability and Yardsticks

- The outperformer needs objective, measurable yardsticks to evaluate and fine-tune his or her progress over time. Two types are needed – those to evaluate how far we have gone, and those that help us evaluate how well we got there.

- The Four Accounts, and their practical implementation, is the measure of distance travelled. Efficiency and leverage evaluate the manner in which you achieved that journey.

- Efficiency comes from learning from others by watching them, reading relevant articles and books and adopting best practices used by friends and colleagues. You should constantly evaluate the way you do things and try to improve your processes.

- The key to leveraged results is having the independence to question other people's assumptions. (This topic is closely linked to Chapter 16, Thinking Outside the Box).

Don't forget the previous chapter: Responsibility

- Responsibility is used in many conflicting and confusing ways in today's society; we therefore provide a clear definition. When used in the context of being responsible for something, we define responsibility as having the power to control and change it. When used in the context of behaving responsibly towards something, we define responsibility as behaving in accordance with your intent.

- Personal responsibility is the ability to control and change yourself, or equivalently it is a contract to act in accordance with your intent. Note that we are separating your self (your intent) from your actions.

- Many people incorrectly see responsibility as a burden. In fact, responsibility is the understanding that you have the power to do something in a situation, about a situation, for an individual or to an individual.

- When you see responsibility as something within your power rather than as something with which to criticise, that shift in focus can actually over time create enthusiasm in you to act responsibly.

Chapter 7
Habits

"*We are what we repeatedly do. Excellence, then, is not an act, but a habit.*"

Aristotle, philosopher

"*A habit is something you can do without thinking – which is why most of us have so many of them.*"

Frank Howard Clark, screenwriter

7.1 Why are habits important?

We all understand on some intuitive level that humans are driven by habits.[59] Nevertheless, most people tend to be shocked by the magnitude of this dependency when they analyse their day-to-day life. Although we have not yet come across a rigorous study that would confirm the belief that habits are one of the biggest determinants of success, there is a wealth of anecdotal evidence suggesting such a conclusion.[60]

Consider your typical weekday. How and when you wake up, what makes up your morning routines, the way you get to work or school, the way you approach your daily tasks, Each of these individual activities can then be broken down into further habits – what is the structure of your 'catch up online' routine? Do you check your email first? How do you process it – randomly, by importance, by time, by people? Where do you read your news? How do you choose what news to read, and how much of it? We could continue de-constructing your daily routines into infinity.

When we really think about our day and realise how many of our activities are habit-driven, it is easy to understand the extent to which habits influence our life, and therefore their importance for the outperformer. Habits are, to put it simply, what either do or do not transform vision into reality.

Given their importance, what do we really mean by 'successful habits'? Successful habits make up everything that happens between our vision and our actions. There are habits which affect how we generate, sort and process ideas. There are habits that influence how our ideas turn into decisions, and decisions into actions.

The better the habits we have – those that create positivity in the accounts – the greater the speed with which we take the actions and the greater the rewards in terms of increasing the accounts.

7.2   Why are our habits frequently self-damaging?

As an experiment, write down three words that you identify with an activity that you do on a habitual basis, examine them and try to change them if required – both the words and the activities.

The move from rationality to self sabotaging habits is gradual, from sleeping as much as our body needs to culminate in us partying until 4am in the morning and going to work/school at 7am. So, what caused that change in the decision-making process? Since we know that a child did not make such decisions, the answer cannot be purely genetic but also to do with external influences. It must be the environment – family, friends, other people, media[61] and culture – that causes poor decision making.

Most of us find it very difficult to change. We confuse the comfort of a habit with comfort in general. When you ask a smoker why he smokes, the answer is often "because it makes me feel better". What he is really saying is that his body and his mind have become dependent on that particular crutch and even thinking of challenging that dependency causes anxiety. Yet most smokers accept that smoking is a habit with long term negative consequences. Long-term negative habits and behaviours tend to act like smoking in that they create a feeling of familiar comfort in us and yet create negative consequences in the long term. We tend to have a natural desire to stay within our 'comfort zones'. But most comfort zones do not increase our long-term happiness generated by increasing our four accounts. All they do is send a message to the mind that the status quo is being observed, which is often not productive but has the comfort of familiarity.

We are naturally resistant to change in general because the status quo has had the feelings of comfort and security associated with it even though it is often to the detriment of happiness and enlightenment in the long term. For example, in certain western countries we have created, and are happy sustaining, an entire culture revolving around the phenomenon of excess alcohol consumption. People feel comfortable with other people who drink and would say "Oh yes, he can let his hair down, he's normal".[62] On the other side, teetotallers[63] are usually seen with suspicion, and called uptight. But thinking rationally, the idea that excess alcohol consumption is a proof of your normality is just completely perverse.

These and other similar old habits come from external influences. They change your thoughts and decision making processes over time and thereby impact your Four Accounts. Creating a belief system backed up by constant verbal validation both by oneself and by other people actually increases our resistance to change. One of the ways you can challenge these ideas is by looking at the very words you use and thereby the signals you are sending to our brains. Advertising demonstrates that words and their connotations influence us on both conscious and subconscious level.[64]

Now look at the words that you wrote down earlier. What you will probably discover is that actually there is great resistance to change these associations. This happens despite the fact that when you rationally examine these habitual activities, they turn out to be irrational – examples include smoking, drinking more than appropriate, thinking cynical and negative thoughts and many others.

Changing your habits is the key to counteracting and reversing the effects of your environment.

7.3   Wage slave's vs. outperformer's habits

The wage slave is modest, or even insecure, about his goals, but extremely confident and wedded to his habits. The outperformer is the opposite; he is ambitious about his goals but humble about his habits. The wage slave is used to the way he does things and refuses to change. The outperformer is the embodiment of flexibility[65] – he is always looking for how to become more efficient between motivation and change, to shorten the time between cause and effect, thought and action.

> *I have experienced this myself at the extreme. I used to be a 100% left-brain, rational, scientifically minded boy who came to the UK from Eastern Europe. I believed that one could 'brute-force' everything through performance, rather than understand that being flexible allows you to find easier, more effective ways of doing things. I was not only an atheist, which I have remained to this day, but also strongly sceptical of any even remotely 'esoteric' or alternative concepts. I was rigid about my diet, ate largely meat and refused to eat vegetables or much fruit. I was using my out-performance to date to prove that my habits were working very well, and did not allow myself or others to question anything.*
>
> *I attribute a large part of the consequent acceleration in my success trajectory to the decision and ability to gradually melt the rigidities of my old self and become someone who is today extremely open to try out practically any new ideas. My old self would shoot down suggestions about how to change my life for the better only because of who or where they came from. Since then, I have trialled and actually adopted a number of habits which would be absolutely inconceivable for me even a few years ago.*
>
> Jan

It is no exaggeration to say that **habits will either make you, as in increase your accounts, or break you, in that nothing moves**. Stagnation is a form of failure; evolution requires a constant change for the better.

The reason habits can either make or break you is that when they become very efficient, they can help encourage your inspiration. If you are stuck in terms of increasing your general motivation, focusing on improving your habits can actually lead to a greater level of success. If low motivation leads to success for someone, that success will end up increasing their motivation, because success makes us happy. An efficient habit can actually thereby lead to improvements in apathetic behaviour.

To this day, despite all of the technological advances of the 20th and 21st century, the human mind is still far more efficient than a computer. It is able to be so because the human mind destroys inactive synapses, and constantly rebuilds itself. We need to become as efficient consciously as we are subconsciously.

Before we look into how to change our habits, let's clarify what constitutes a good habit. The point of habits is to turn our inspiration and vision into actions as quickly, effectively, and efficiently as possible. And the best way to measure this is again through our accounts, as described in the earlier chapter on measurability. Good habits are therefore those that help us increase our Four Accounts in the most efficient and leveraged way, given our intent.

7.4   How to change your habits

Changing your habits is one of the most difficult things you will ever encounter in your life. There is a reason why so many people fail every day, week, month and year to stick to their new success creating habits, regardless of whether these are to do with work ethics, exercise, sleep, diet, smoking, alcohol or anything else.

Fortunately, we know a lot more about the human brain today than we did even a few decades ago. Scientists and outperformers have both contributed to our understanding of how the brain works, what are its strengths and how to use them, as well as what are its flaws and how to correct for these flaws. The purpose of this chapter is to equip you with the most powerful strategy for changing your habits so that you have much better odds of success.

1. Always focus on one habit at a time, except if the two (three, four…) are closely related

It has been shown again and again that if you try to change too many things in your life, you will almost certainly fail. The reason why so many New Year's resolutions never live to see the end of January is that people try to change everything in their lives at once. We know that a) it is difficult to change our habits b) our brain finds it difficult to focus on too many different objectives.

Whatever strategy you therefore adopt for the actual process of changing your habits, you should always focus on one task only. There is a single exception to this rule – if there are two habits in your life that are very closely related in any way, it may make sense to tackle them both at once. There are a few notorious examples of this.

It is often helpful to tackle your diet and exercise at the same time – if you convince yourself to replace your usual fast food snack with a salad for lunch, you will not want to waste that effort by not going to the gym in the evenings. Conversely, when you get back from the gym, you are likely to think twice about ordering pizza or bingeing on chocolate when you remember how hard you worked on the treadmill.

Similarly, if you are a smoker and a heavy coffee drinker, your chances of success are much higher if you give up both at once, or for example only drink coffee in an environment where smoking simply is not an option. We know that certain links in our brain are extremely strong, and the urge to have a cigarette with their cup of coffee is one of the major reasons for smokers failing to change this habit.

There are a number of other examples, including alcohol consumption and bingeing on fast food. To put it simply, if you believe that changing two of your habits at once is likely to make it easier to change both, you should consider breaking this rule.

2. It takes a month to change a habit

Again, as we mention in other parts of this book, there is unfortunately only one good way of telling our brain that something is important – repetition. By spending a month on a single habit, you will be able to convince your brain that this is something that is important to you. Even more importantly, you should become so used to the new habit that it becomes a part of your 'default' behaviour pattern.

The purpose of any habit-changing exercise is to get to a point where you can start focusing on something else without putting your newly acquired habit at risk of reverting back to its original state. Many agree that one month is the best period to achieve such a goal – not too short so that things would revert back afterwards, but still sufficiently short to allow you to tackle a number of things every year. Again, there will be exceptions to this rule, particularly to do with certain addictions such as smoking.

3. Experimentation is good

There are a number of behavioural patterns that explain why we are so afraid of change. For example, endowment effect is a well documented bias that makes us place a greater value on something we already own relatively to the same thing that we are able to buy.

In other words, most people would never pay $1000 for a bottle of fine wine. If they, however, own the same bottle of wine because they won it in some competition, they would not sell it for $1000. From a rational, economic point of view, the two behavioural patterns are inconsistent – we should either prefer the $1000 in cash, or the bottle of wine, all the time.

The outperformer understands the way his mind works, and takes advantage of it. What do we mean by experimentation when it comes to habits then? It is actually quite simple – just start seeing new habits as experiments, things you would like to try, rather than permanent shifts in your life.

It is not very appealing, especially to a young person, to decide not to binge on junk food ever again. But what if you just decided to stay away from junk food for a month, and then see if you like this new habit or not? This makes it a lot easier to accept for the mind, and hence your odds of success are much higher.

4. Time-neutral habits are easier to change

What do we mean by that? Time neutral habits are to do with changing the way you do certain things, rather than introducing new things into your life. Deciding to start going to the gym three times a week is a new routine you have to introduce into your life. Deciding to use stairs rather than lifts whenever possible does not require (almost) any extra time or introducing anything new into your life. It is therefore a time neutral habit.

Similarly, deciding to drink water rather than soft drinks whenever possible is quite easy – you do not need to change anything, just order water when appropriate. This makes it impossible for you to use time as an excuse – you cannot argue as easily as when you tell yourself that you could not go to the gym because you had a school project to finish.

5. Make it as easy for yourself as possible

This point is almost always way too neglected, but can make all the difference. Changing habits is a hard task as it stands, so why make it harder for yourself? When are you more likely to develop a healthy exercise habit – if your gym is next door or if it involves a 30 minute trek by public transport? When are you more likely to start eating healthy food – if your fridge is full of pre-made food and ice cream, or if you stuff your kitchen with fruit and vegetables?

6. Make yourself accountable

Write things down – it really is quite simple. If you want to become fitter, start writing down how much exercise you do each day, including how far/much you run, cycle, swim, or what weights you lift. If you want to get better grades, start writing down how much time you spend on each subject every week, including what do you do in that time.

7. Create positive pressure

Have you decided to get straight As in your examinations, or to lose 30 pounds? Tell your parents, family, trusted friends and teachers about it. Telling everyone what you want to achieve makes it a lot harder to fail. You would need to explain to them why you failed. Most of us hate being seen as failures, or explaining why we screw up. Creating positive pressure and external expectations is a good way to give ourselves an extra dose of motivation.

Alternatively, do something else that will create the same positive pressure. Do you want to become fitter? Book and pay in advance for an adventurous mountain-hiking expedition you have always wanted to do. Do you want to lose weight? Plan and book a beach holiday with your best friends, including the guy or girl you have had a crush on for the last two years.

There is nothing complicated or sophisticated about the seven strategies outlined above. Nevertheless, adopting at least some of them will multiply your chances of success in changing your habits many times over.

Key Takeaways: Habits

- Habits drive your life, and therefore have significant impact on your success. The habits we pursue are often the key difference between successful and unsuccessful people. If you do some specific things habitually then success can become very easy.

- The better habits you have (i.e. the more helpful your habits are to creating positivity in your Four Accounts), the greater the speed with which you take the important steps and the quicker you can increase your accounts.

- Your habits can be self-damaging, and most people find it difficult to change. This is a product of environment; there are multiple effects at work that make getting rid of old habits and acquiring new ones difficult.

- There are specific strategies you can adopt that significantly improve your chances of success in changing your habits. They are not complicated but can make all the difference.

- The wage slave is modest, or even insecure, about his goals, but extremely confident and wedded to his habits. The outperformer is the opposite; ambitious about his goals but humble about his habits.

Don't forget the previous chapter: Measurability and Yardsticks

- The outperformer needs objective, measurable yardsticks to evaluate and fine-tune his or her progress over time. Two types are needed – those to evaluate how far we have gone, and those that help us evaluate how well we got there.

- The Four Accounts, and their practical implementation, is the measure of distance travelled. Efficiency and leverage evaluate the manner in which you achieved that journey.

- Efficiency comes from learning from others by watching them, reading relevant articles and books and adopting best practices used by friends and colleagues. You should constantly evaluate the way you do things and try to improve your processes.

- The key to leveraged results is having the independence to question other people's assumptions. (This topic is closely linked to Chapter 16, Thinking Outside the Box).

Chapter 8
Drive

"If you want to build a ship, do not drum up people to collect wood and do not assign them tasks and work, but rather teach them to long for the endless immensity of the sea."

Antoine de Saint-Exupery, writer and aviator

"Look into your past, and see what keeps you up all night ... or gets you bouncing out of bed first thing in the morning, ... or gets you so intensely focused that hours fly by and you do not even notice."

Derek Sivers, entrepreneur

8.1 How to create inspiration

There are two roadblocks that make it particularly difficult to become inspired: poor physical health, and poor mental health. Let's focus on mental health first as it is much easier for most of us to change. The best way to tell if one has poor mental health, and to actually reverse this situation, is by starting to develop some positivity in one's mental account. In particular, there are three habits that we have found to be highly beneficial for creating inspiration, and igniting a positive virtuous cycle in general.

Firstly, read an inspiring book or watch an inspiring programme every day. This will slowly lead to a desire to watch and discuss only things that produce the same effect. Sadly, there are some regrettable ideas prevalent in today's society: all too often, great art is meant to make you feel cathartic or shocked; horror movies are a popular entertainment – sadistic, violent behaviour is something to watch and enjoy; misogynistic and/or violence based lyrics are venerated as cool; many great works of fiction depict betrayal, loss, rejection and unreciprocated love as normal, and often inevitable, in one's life.

Such fallacies will slowly begin to feel as unhealthy for the person who daily reads or watches something inspiring as for the super healthy athlete who starts suddenly drinking alcohol and eating junk food.

Secondly, try to interact with one inspiring individual every day. Being around an inspiring person[66], if done regularly, will change the belief in you about how your friends, your work colleagues and your family should really treat you. When you become used to an inspiring individual, become happy being in their company, and become used to the uplifting nature of the interaction, the desire will arise to emulate that more and more in all your other relationships.

It will become the equivalent of the adrenaline rush from physical exercise. More and more, you will make logical decisions to step away from dysfunctional friendships. Instead, over time, there will be an increased desire to be in groups that are inspiring and nurturing.

In the fullness of time you will be the one who drives the inspirational dynamic in a group. Then you will have come full circle – from starting by being the one looking for inspirational relationships to finding those relationships in the middle to being the one always instigating that dynamic of inspiration and mutual nurturing in the end. You will start to feel inspired, as we do, by the improvements in those you are mentoring.

Thirdly, take time for at least 15 minutes twice a day, and often take a few minutes every 3–4 hours, to just sit and think.[67] During those periods, you should only think about those things in your life that are positive, in the sense that you feel happy visualising them. Calm your mind so that you can make more rational and ultimately inspirational choices.[68]

The calmness, if it is pursued effectively – i.e. it brings about that emotional state of calm and happiness and peace – will lead you to understand that being with oneself can be a positive, nurturing thing and it does not have to be a place of anxiety and stress. A lot of people avoid being by themselves because it makes them feel depressed.

It is true that being with yourself in a bad way (sitting by yourself thinking negative thoughts) can be detrimental, but being with yourself in a good way creates calmness, peace and – this is very important – can actually be where inspiration arises. Many people, Einstein included, have attributed their time alone in quiet reflection as being the most productive part of their day. It allows one to get a sense of perspective on one's difficulties, and a sense of balance, serenity and cohesion in the way one views one's life.

**These habits, if they are routinely observed, will slowly
start to reverse the apathetic comfort zones** that we become
so used to because all three of them will reverse certain key
beliefs that have become a rigid perspective in us. Over time,
these new habits will create huge rewards by becoming the
foundation for more inspirational thinking and better decision making.

If you imagine that today your thinking is built around the
beliefs that junk food should be part of your regular diet,
exercise is sacrifice, best company are friends who are football
hooligans or bitchy girlfriends and that horror movies are the
best form of entertainment – then it is hardly surprising to
realise that there is a deep sense of resistance to taking uplifting action in you.

If, on the other hand, you follow the new habits outlined in
this chapter, as well as the health and fitness habits outlined
later, **you will start to believe that anything is possible**.
Very importantly, this will make perfect logical sense to your
left-brain, because you will have given your mind plenty of
evidence that this is indeed the case.

1. You will start to believe that physically you can do
   everything – because you have actually been practising a
   healthy, demanding regime and eating well.

2. You will start to believe that you can have really good
   ideas, because you stayed calm and allowed those ideas
   to happen.

3. You will start to believe that there are friends out there
   who can help you with your goals – whether personal or
   professional – because you have met and interacted with
   a number of inspiring people.

4. Finally, you will start to believe that any work you do can
   succeed and any human achievement is possible, because
   you have read about it in a number of inspiring books,
   and seen it in a number of inspiring programmes.

What happens then is that these new habits will create a level of positivity which finally shifts our human apathetic nature.

8.2   How to avoid vicious circles and blaming others

One of the most powerful concepts we have introduced in this book is that of virtuous cycles and vicious circles. To remind you, we talked about how underperformance in one of the accounts can lead to underperformance in others, creating a negative feedback loop that leads to depression, and underperformance. Inspiration is actually one of best ways of getting out of a depression cycle.[69] This chapter explains how it can be used to help you get out of such a cycle.

A great way of creating a healthy current emotional state, one that allows you to become inspired, is by constantly telling yourself that the past is ancient history and you just do your best now. Inspiration is often burdened. Even if it arises, we refuse to recognise it because we immediately drown it with our negativity. "Well, great business idea but I had a few businesses ideas before – they all failed." or "Oh, other people have always shot down my creativity in the past." or "I just feel tired all the time."

What is often interesting is that it is not the case that people do not get any inspiring ideas, but there comes a point for most people when any inspiring ideas are just shot down so quickly that the mind adapts and stops trying to persuade us of their efficacy. One of the most common negative thought patterns that human beings get into is that there is no point in getting inspired because you will never be able to do anything about it. This is a tough one to crack and the way to do this is through the new habits described in the previous chapter.

The human mind is a fascinating, incredibly productive tool. In children there are many more neural pathways before the age of five than in older people. The mind has been found to be extremely efficient and anything it does not use over time it will allow to decay; on the other hand, pathways that are used often will be nurtured more.[70] Once you realise that your brain is constantly creating neural pathways to accommodate your habits and comfort zones, you can begin to take advantage of this process.

It may well be the case that in the beginning, you need exogenous inputs and stimuli in order to start habits that will then change or recreate the neural pathways[71] that lead to inspiration. Conversely, if you walk away from negative old habits, the neural pathways that always bring about the negative sentiment ("It is not going to happen.", "Never going to work out." etc.) will then become unused, and decay over time.

This is a tough task to accomplish, and it is one – like all truly hard challenges for prosperity and success – which requires something that is very easy and very difficult at the same time, the habitual practice of the opposite. As we said in the chapter on habits, many believe that it takes 30 days to form a new habit. This is one habit that would be worth spending 30 months on; the habit of refusing to focus on the thought that nothing you do matters. Learning to walk away from that thought and instead look for enthusiasm, inspiration etc. is a true challenge, but also one capable of generating a massive payoff.

At a behavioural level one of the worst ways that people get into depression is by spending a lot of time blaming others.[72] Blame is a powerful force in the world that is used by individuals to escape responsibility for what they do have power over in their own lives. One of the greatest areas where people tend to blame society is for the lack of opportunities we have been given to educate and better ourselves.

This is actually something that both of us are very passionate about. Muzaffar felt very strongly in his twenties that life was not fair – while he was incredibly blessed in life by going to the best schools and universities and being taught a lot of life skills far beyond any state school curriculum, others did not get the same chances. Now in his forties, writing this book has been his way of taking responsibility for it, by giving advice on these life skills to level out the playing field.

Jan's story, detailed in at the beginning of the book, has been an incredible example of what can be achieved by someone coming from a very humble background without any of the privileges that Muzaffar or others had.

Everyone who reads this book now has to admit that they have more clarity about what are the needed life skills, both for school or university and for the workplace. Furthermore, they know how to develop these required skills. Similarly, while we live in an imperfect world with unequal opportunities, it does not mean that there is nothing you can do, and that you can use a low starting point to justify low underachievement. It is now up to the reader to go out and implement some of the things in this book, rather than continuing to blame society for perceived elitism, sexism, or racism, for his or her lack of advancement in life. While that may be the case to some degree, it is rarely the only explanation, and there is always an opportunity to change things for the better.

Key Takeaways: Drive

- It is possible to initiate virtuous cycles through exogenous influences. Firstly, read an inspiring book or watch an inspiring programme every day. This will lead to a desire to watch and discuss only things that produce the same effect.

- Interact every day with one individual who is inspiring to you. Being around an inspiring person, if done regularly, will change the belief in you about how your friends, your work colleagues and your family should really treat you.

- Take at least 15 minutes twice a day, and often take a few minutes every 3–4 hours, to just sit quietly and try to feel calm. It will help you calm your mind so that you can make rational and ultimately inspirational choices.

- These habits, if routinely observed, will slowly start to reverse the apathetic comfort zones that it is easy to become used to. All three of them will reverse certain key beliefs that have become a rigid perspective in you.

Don't forget the previous chapter: Habits

- Habits drive your life, and therefore have significant impact on your success. The habits we pursue are often the key difference between successful and unsuccessful people. If you do some specific things habitually then success can become very easy.

- The better habits you have (i.e. the more helpful your habits are to creating positivity in your Four Accounts), the greater the speed with which you take the important steps and the quicker you can increase your accounts.

- Your habits can be self-damaging, and most people find it difficult to change. This is a product of environment; there are multiple effects at work that make getting rid of old habits and acquiring new ones difficult.

- There are specific strategies you can adopt that significantly improve your chances of success in changing your habits. They are not complicated but can make all the difference.

- The wage slave is modest, or even insecure, about his goals, but extremely confident and wedded to his habits. The outperformer is the opposite; ambitious about his goals but humble about his habits.

Chapter 9
Doing What You Love

"Find something you love to do and you'll never have to work a day in your life."

Harvey MacKay, businessman and columnist

"Your time is limited, so do not waste it living someone else's life. Do not be trapped by dogma – which is living with the results of other people's thinking. Do not let the noise of other's opinions drown out your own inner voice. And most important, have the courage to follow your heart and intuition. They somehow already know what you truly want to become. Everything else is secondary."

Steve Jobs, CEO of Apple Inc

9.1 How to discover what you love?

When asked about what they love doing, many people will talk about how they love to play computer games, watch certain programmes, go out with their friends and party, smoke or drink etc. If you were, however, to sit down and truly observe yourself you would realise that actually these are things that have become habits over time. They have become parts of your comfort zones, rather than a source of genuine enjoyment.

For most people, watching horror movies adds nothing to their sense of productivity, long term happiness or to their positive view of the world. Most people actually find themselves fatigued and drained after watching TV for a period of time. This is why it is really important to be able to distance yourself from the way you perceive the world and start differentiating between the happiness of comfort zones and real happiness. This exercise is what allows you to realise what it actually is that you love to do.[73] You will discover that what you actually love to do are things that increase your Four Accounts without causing any decreases in one of them in any way.

One of the habits we talked about earlier is quiet self-reflection. This is one of the best opportunities for discovering what you actually enjoy doing. This is the time when you really need to sit and reflect on whether you enjoy things because they are in you comfort zone or whether you enjoy them because they are bringing increases in the Four Accounts in the short, medium and long term. That distinction and the awareness of it are very important to the evolution of the outperformer.

Finally, experimentation, which we repeatedly encourage throughout this book, is a proven way of finding something great by chance. Most people are 'sheep' and often do what is popular, surviving by adaptation and conformity. Experimentation breaks right through that.

9.2   How to sustain and enhance your enthusiasm

Most people do not actually have a problem with motivating themselves in the short-term. You probably had multiple experiences when a movie, a book, a friend or just a sudden burst of self-reflection elevated your motivation levels and you felt like you are finally on track to conquer the world – or at least become a straight A-grade student, lose 20 pounds or create a million dollar business.

Unfortunately, these bursts of motivation tend to last hours, days or at best weeks for most young people, only for them to slowly descend into their former reality of repeated failures later. The inability to sustain enthusiasm for longer periods of time is one of the prime reasons for repeated failures and under-achievement. We have touched upon some of the more abstract and strategic reasons in the chapter on vision. On the tactical level, the single biggest mistake is having a bad strategy or even worse no strategy at all.

There are a number of behavioural, evolutionary and psychological reasons for why this is indeed the case. Fortunately, understanding these reasons means that we can create certain methods of correcting for them, and hopefully utilise these to sustain our inspiration, motivation and drive for longer. The following suggestions are not complete or absolute solutions – they are simply tools that have been shown to help.

1. Writing things down

Write stuff down. This is the simplest and best piece of advice we can give you on goal setting. Do you want to lose weight? Record what and when you eat, and when and how much you exercise. Do you want to improve your grades? Record when and how you revise. Do you want to save money? Use a service that helps you get a better feeling for your expenditure.

Your left brain is incapable of monitoring and evaluating anything that is not measured. If you do not write down your expenditures, your idea of what you spend your money on will be driven by a few intuitive, anecdotal examples – you buying cinema tickets yesterday, you buying DVDs last week, you buying those shoes earlier this month etc.

At first sight, the time needed to monitor everything may seem excessive – in reality, it never totals more than a few minutes every day. Hardly a big deal if such practice can help you become more efficient in activities that take hours.

2. Visualise it

Once you write down the goal, you should try to visualise it and make it very real and tangible. How do you think the best athletes motivate themselves to endure the years of demanding training? They imagine themselves standing on the podium with that gold Olympic medal over and over and over again, until it becomes a very real, tangible idea.

Some people actually like to get a picture or some other physical object that represents their goal and carry it with them. When they are working towards their goal and get distracted or start to procrastinate, they just pull out this object. This then activates a certain part of their brain which retrieves memories and feelings linked to their goal.

There is one simple way of telling our brain that something is important – repetition. Just think about how you revise. By visualising your goals again and again, you are telling your brain that this is important, and also turning an abstract idea into something very real.

3. Focus on tangible things, not abstract concepts

The human brain is quite good in handling abstract concepts, but it is even more powerful when it comes to real objects that interact directly with our senses – images, sounds, smells, tastes, touches. The reason why the brain behaves in this way is that when you think about something closely associated with a certain sense, the brain works in reverse. If you imagine the picture of a rose, your brain will project the smell of rose onto the part of your brain that normally deals with smells. This also works the other way round.

It is not easy for your brain to closely relate itself to the notion of being healthy and beautiful, or to the idea of topping your year at university, or with the idea of being wealthy. If your goal is similarly abstract, the best way to increase your motivation and make it more permanent is to turn them into tangible things.

Do you think athletes imagine 'winning the race' when they need to motivate themselves? No. They imagine what it feels and sounds like to finish first in front of tens of thousands of people shouting, cheering and celebrating their success.

Do you want to top your year? Imagine receiving the awards and respect this would create, the scholarships you would receive, the jobs you could get and the universities you could now apply for if you wanted to do another degree. Do you want to become healthy and beautiful? Imagine how you would feel amongst your friends, or walking into a room full of strangers.

Do you want to become wealthy? Do not think about an amount of money. Think about the lifestyle and freedom this would bring you. Imagine the home you could create, places you could visit, hobbies you could pick up, service you could receive, tedious things you would no longer need to do yourself.

This sounds really simple, but empirical evidence from the world's leading outperformers across different fields of human activity confirms that practising and perfecting this habit is a key to success.

4. Experience those tangible things

The effect described above can be enhanced even further if you can sample the experience you are trying to achieve. This will usually be quite difficult, as by definition, the dreams you aspire to tend to be difficult to experience. In most cases, however, there are ways of getting around this problem.

It is difficult to sample the experience of winning an Olympic race, but you can probably compete in a regional or national competition, particularly if you are in a junior age group, in order to simulate a similar experience. It is difficult to sample the life of an accomplished professor, but you can work really hard on a given project and sample the experience of being the best in your year, school or country.

Why do you think the world's leading universities spend a lot of effort on getting successful and wealthy alumni in front of their students, or even to mentor them? This makes the entire experience very real to these students, so the visualisation of it becomes easier. Internships work in a very similar way, whether they are at investment banks, law firms, accountancies, management consulting firms or in industry. Part of the value of internships, especially the first year insight programmes, is that you can see the lifestyle towards which you are aspiring.

That way the life you aspire to feels much more tangible to you rather than a distant hope. The more tangible it is, the more you can see yourself living this future. This makes it emotionally easier to work harder now – it acts as a powerful motivator and you bring your enthusiasm along to the party.

5. Monitor your progress

Understand and accept that no serious achievement in this world is a product of one burst of motivation, one afternoon, or one month. Paul Buchheit, the creator of Gmail and one of the leading figures of the Web 2.0 revolution, actually wrote an excellent piece titled *Overnight success takes a long time*[74]. This title has a lot of truth in it – even the things which you may perceive as having been an overnight success frequently had a lot of work done on them beneath the surface.

You should therefore expect any serious goal to take time, and require effort. This does not mean, however, that you should blindly work towards this goal without regards for your emotions. One of the most important things you should always observe is consistency of your actions – a person is not truly inspired if they are not consistent. Inconsistency means that you are coming from some negative emotion towards your goal – fear, anxiety or something else. In that case, you need to go back and figure out what is happening.

6. Last but not least, set the rules.

One of the concepts that have been found to bring clarity to the mind, thereby leading to inspiration, is the doctrine of the 'Four Agreements' used by the Toltec[75], the mythical ancestors of the Aztecs who lived in today's Mexico in pre-Columbian times. The agreements are as follows:

a) Be impeccable with your word

Truth is one of the strongest ways of creating and sustaining inspiration. People, including our self, respond well to an honest person, and can be enthused more easily. You have to tell the truth to yourself otherwise your self-saboteur will not believe you and will wear you down with attack thoughts.

For example, do not promise yourself a big night out at the end of two weeks of intensive training and dieting if you know you will not allow yourself to actually do it. You will now be less likely to follow through with the work out as well. Same goes for your interaction with others.

b) Do not take anything personally

However anyone treats you has no reflection on you. No

trauma justifies shutting down in the medium and long term. However anyone criticises you does not mean that you are beyond correction. You just have to connect with the good in yourself and then you can always go back. This is a very powerful way of inspiring people or yourself; a person who is not petty is more inspiring than someone who is, because his personal nature does not distract from his words but actually adds to them.

c) Do not make assumptions

For example, do not make assumptions about people based on their past performance. Give them room to grow, no one is static. This is powerful, because it allows you to see people as constantly changing, allowing you to avoid pigeonholing people, but rather seeing them for who they are.

d) Always do your best

This, in many ways, is the most powerful agreement. It allows you to get out of a vicious circle, to change your reality, to choose to be happy. Ignoring the pull of "I did not do it [exercise, work, studying] for a week, so I will not do it for another week, it is all lost anyway." You can start doing your best right **now** regardless of your past. You always have the power in the present moment to change the trajectory of your success. You can shift from going backwards to racing towards excellence.

Asking "Do I want to do my best in this particular endeavour?" is a fantastic way of staying true to your vision. Does this endeavour make me want to do my best, or does this endeavour only make me want to do enough to pass? This will tell you a lot about whether you are truly inspired, or if it is just a fear-based motivation. This is a fantastic yardstick. Do you want to come in at 9 and leave at 5, or do you really care?

Key Takeaways: Doing What You Love

- There is a difference between enjoying an activity because it is in your comfort zone and genuinely deriving pleasure from it.

- The outperformer understands this difference and its long-run impact on his or her life. It pays to focus your attention on making this distinction early, and changing your habits accordingly.

- Sustaining your enthusiasm is something which you can significantly influence using a few simple to use strategies. This is what outperformers across disciplines and across the world do.

- It is much easier for your brain to be motivated if the eventual goal is tangible, and if it impacts your senses. Translate your abstract goals into related visual images, smells, sounds, think about them often, and make it clear to your brain in this way that they are important.

Don't forget the previous chapter: Drive

- It is possible to initiate virtuous cycles through exogenous influences. Firstly, read an inspiring book or watch an inspiring programme every day. This will lead to a desire to watch and discuss only things that produce the same effect.

- Interact every day with one individual who is inspiring to you. Being around an inspiring person, if done regularly, will change the belief in you about how your friends, your work colleagues and your family should really treat you.

- Take at least 15 minutes twice a day, and often take a few minutes every 3–4 hours, to just sit quietly and try to feel calm. It will help you calm your mind so that you can make rational and ultimately inspirational choices.

- These habits, if routinely observed, will slowly start to reverse the apathetic comfort zones that it is easy to become used to. All three of them will reverse certain key beliefs that have become a rigid perspective in you.

Chapter 10

Health and Fitness

"Pain is temporary. It may last a minute, or an hour, or a day, or a year, but eventually it will subside and something else will take its place. If I quit, however, it lasts forever."

Lance Armstrong, cyclist

"Sometimes the most productive thing one can do is to sleep."

Unknown

10.1   Why are health and fitness important?

Our physical account, that is our health and fitness, is undoubtedly and without question the one account capable of unleashing a brutal, ferocious spiral that is either virtuous or vicious. Most of you will be aware of numerous examples, both from your personal networks and public figures, where sudden improvement or deterioration in health and fitness lead to a more fundamental change for better or worse.

What is also interesting is how closely inspiration and enthusiasm are connected to our energy, i.e. the feeling of vitality within our body as certain ideas come up. It is therefore extremely important to develop habits that lead to consistently high energy levels, and conversely to monitor our energy levels in order to detect first signs of any potential problems. Observing our physical energy levels is a very good yardstick for detecting if there is problem with our lifestyle or our inspiration.

If you cannot be inspired to do anything, then look to see what is going on with your physical body. There are physical reasons why people get depressed.[76] If you are feeling tired all the time, you are more likely to actually feel scared, dislike your job and create a vicious circle. But if you are feeling optimistic and energised, you are more likely to feel inspired by looking to do the next positive thing. So when it's functioning well, your body can become an active force for inspiration.

Given the authors' backgrounds in financial markets and the City in general, lifestyles of people who work in investment banking, law and other similar professions make for interesting case studies. For those of you unaware of the environment, junior employees in these professions will frequently work 15–18 hours a day, 7 days a week and even see this as a badge of honour.

The way that many bankers and other young professionals, and in fact many students, cope with that level of stress is by overindulging in things that increase one's adrenaline, giving them short bursts of focus. The primary ways that they do that is by using caffeine based products[77] and, in a minority of cases, harmful drugs that are used are stimulants. Once the need for stimulants ends they would then compensate with alcohol, various feel-good substances and other harmful drugs to vent the built-up tension.

On both sides of the equation, the stimulant and the relaxant, there is overindulgence. Both have a long-term negative effect on the body. Indeed, one of the best and most objective ways of recognising if you are treating your body negatively is to see how much physical exercise you are doing. When harmful stimulant use becomes routine, physical exercise is often the first thing to go.

This comes back to the difference between a vision and an objective. The reason so many people feel comfortable doing long-term damage to their body is that they see life as a series of objectives, and therefore feel that they can make short-term sacrifices. The problem is that one objective gets replaced by another, and a short-term sacrifice becomes a long-term one. Moreover, health works in a cumulative manner, and long-term damage is often difficult to undo.

Fortunately, there are a number of people who have proven that working long hours in a stressful environment is no excuse for leading an unhealthy lifestyle. There is a difference between high quantity and high quality sleep. Most people sleep 'badly', or at least 'inefficiently'. Both of the authors have worked 100+ hour weeks using the exact opposite of the conventional strategy – a combination of healthy diet, high quality sleep and physical exercise. Amongst other things, such a strategy means that one actually has energy to work during those hours, rather than just keep surviving.

10.2 Diet

'Health and fitness' is today associated with exercise first, diet second, sleep third. In fact, the three factors are equally important[78], and there is a great deal of interaction between them. What they have in common is the degree to which common sense gets ignored in favour of flawed commercial interest. In particular, an entire industry has grown and prospered by providing dieting advice, products and materials, when questions about what constitutes healthy diet could mostly by answered by a 15 year old with common sense and a few basic facts.

Eat real food.[79] **Drink plenty of fluids, mostly water.** The importance of hydration for energy levels and focus cannot be overemphasised.[80] And what do we mean by real food? Real food grows and dies. It is not heavily processed by machines, and rots rather quickly. It is not prepared in the microwave. It does not come sealed in air tight plastic, tin, cardboard or any other box for that matter. It does not have an ingredient label with nutrition breakdown. It does not claim to be healthy, or anything else for that matter. It is usually not branded.

Unprocessed vegetables, fruit, fish and meat should form the majority of your diet. There are conflicting views on grains and dairy, and experts still seem to disagree on their suitability for our diet. If you are interested, we would recommend digging into the issue deeper in order to form your own opinion.

Eat your meals in a way that mirrors your energy needs. What is the typical diet for the large majority of the Western world today? Breakfast is non-existent or cereal with milk, and hence not nutritionally adequate. Lunch is typically a small sandwich eaten in a hurry. Hardly the brain food required at the peak of our productivity. Completely irrationally, we then top things off with a calorie-rich, meat-based dinner at 8–9pm, about 2–3 hours before going to sleep.

Compare this to the amount of energy your body needs throughout the day. High in the morning to get you started, consistent throughout the day and then progressively less in the evening. What this means is that for the large majority of the population, the body does not have enough energy to work efficiently when it is needed, i.e. during the day. Conversely, the body has excess energy when it does not need it, i.e. when we are sleeping, and so logically it stores all that energy in the form of excess fat.

Last but not least, as with all habits, do not be afraid to experiment. Productivity writers and researchers have popularised the concept of trials of various lengths to establish if certain habits prove beneficial, and this applies particularly to food. Provided that you do this within reason and always research properly the medical implications of the diet you might decide to try, experimentation is an excellent tool to determine the effect of different foods on your health.

The reason why the nutrition industry has prospered in a completely perverse way is that while our environment has changed monumentally since the Stone Age, our instincts responsible for food intake have not. Eating as much of that mammoth rump as you can possibly squeeze into your stomach makes a great deal of sense if you just got lucky and may starve for another couple of months. Stuffing your face with as much of that Big Mac and Fries as possible makes less sense when there's a McDonald's on every corner.

It is no surprise that people continue looking for the miraculous solution that would allow them to continue bingeing on junk food and then take a pill that would take care of everything else. The reality is that while there are no easy solutions, it is actually not that difficult to change our habits, including the diet.

> *I was brought up in the Czech Republic by parents who love gastronomy, cooking and good food. This meant that I grew up on two hot, home-made meat-based meals a day, and refused to eat practically all vegetables until about 16 years of age. My coffee consumption peaked at 15 cups a day at one point. I quit drinking coffee 'cold-turkey' without any withdrawal problems about two years ago. In the last twelve months, I went from being a meat enthusiast to vegetarian, to vegan, to raw foodist, back to eating meat and am still continuing to experiment. At every stage of this journey, I had little problem in convincing my taste buds to like the new diet.*
>
> Jan

The reason why most people struggle is because of their laziness to research and explore the new diet. It takes effort to discover good recipes and restaurants if you switch to vegetarian, vegan or even a raw food diet. It is much easier to order in Chinese or eat out.

Our taste is surprisingly easy to override, especially when you manage to visualise the long-term damaging effect of certain foods on your health. To put it simply, if you keep explaining to your brain what that greasy junk food is going to do to your health in 20 years, your brain will eventually catch up and adjust accordingly.

To make it absolutely clear – we are not advocating any particular diet here, except for common sense. Neither of us claim to have the expertise to make such judgements – indeed, the theory on what food is best for the human body is changing constantly (depending on who is sponsoring the research, sadly). What we are saying is that following common sense – that is, eating real foods, eating slowly when you are hungry and stopping before you are full, drinking plenty of water and adjusting your nutrition intake to your daily cycle – accounts for the large majority of health, fitness and energy gains that are available through changing our diet, much in the spirit of the 80–20 rule.

Finally, the body itself should not be disregarded as a partner in terms of the feedback it gives you. In the old Indian yogic tradition, for example, the most important thing when preparing food was taste, so a lot of spices were used. The belief back then was that when something tasted nice, the body digested it better. This is why there should be a sense– whatever diet one has – that one should find it tasty.

As we described in the chapter on love, there has been too much of an emphasis on people using diet as a way of emotional punishment. This is certainly not helpful as it means that one will eventually go off the diet. Those who use food as a rod on their back end up having cravings for chocolates, ice cream etc.

The best way of not storing up an addictive relationship with food is to make sure you know why you find whatever food you eat tasty, rather than having an unconscious preference for foods with high quantities of salt, sugar and fat.[81] This is the best defence against having cravings for foods. It is also the best way of retraining the mind because if you find certain foods very tasty then you will change to them; conversely, if you do not like your new diet then the mind will always think "I am being punished" and will cry out for 'comfort' foods.

10.3 Sleep

It is unfortunate, and in many ways ironic, that sleep – **the single most efficient way of revitalising our body and mind**[82] – is often perceived as the ultimate enemy by both students and junior professionals. What then ends up happening is a pointless race to cut down to 7, 6, 5, 4, 3 hours of sleep per day (with a few all-nighters thrown in for good measure), and in many cases people start bragging about this to their friends as a way of demonstrating their busy-ness and commitment to work or studies.

The healthy approach to sleep is the exact opposite. The way to reduce one's sleep demands and free up time for other things is to see sleep as your partner and best ally. The practical way of doing so is based on behaving in a loving way towards your body in order to ensure that we need as little sleep as possible, and that the sleep we get is of the highest possible quality.

The way to reduce the amount of sleep your body needs is to reduce the damage you do to it every day. Sleep is ultimately a repair mode for our body, and so the less there is to be repaired and rejuvenated, the less sleep we end up needing. If your evenings are spent smoking and drinking too much alcohol and your then top things off with a kebab on the way home, it will inevitably be more difficult for your body to fix things, and the body will take longer to do so.

How to make sure that the sleep you get is of maximum quality is a bit more complicated, and still a subject of debate by both researchers and the general public. There are, however, certain principles that seem to be widely supported. In particular, many people find that following the sun cycle (going to bed early and waking up early) reduces the amount of sleep they need, and increases their energy levels.

There are a number of other techniques that are still the subject of debate regarding their effect on sleep quality and quantity. As with your diet, the best advice here is to experiment within reason, and try to figure out what works best for you. A technique that seems to be particularly popular involves the use of soothing music, both to fall asleep quickly and to keep you in the deeper, most relaxing stages of sleep for longer.[83] Using a gentle alarm clock and making sure that you spend some time exposed to natural light shortly after waking up both tend to increase your energy levels throughout the day.

10.4 Exercise

Exercise has again been mistakenly perceived, like food, as an area in life that is a punishment and sacrifice for ourselves, whereas both can – and should – be highly enjoyable. Making exercise enjoyable is actually the key to developing positive habits in this area. In fact, exercise is one of the prime examples of life skills that the best schools instil in their students, going back to our comment many chapters ago. The best schools are very good in turning sports into enjoyable activities.

Boredom with the actual exercise is one of the primary reasons for why people drop out. One of the big reasons why people who leave school or university stop exercising is that one suddenly needs to make an effort to be able to participate in team sports. The process of physical strain without any social reward makes it a chore. The second is to do with time – we are apparently simply too busy to make time in our schedules to exercise properly. Fortunately, Barack Obama has provided us with the ultimate answer to such excuses. As many commentators noted recently, there was both a visible change in Mr Obama's physique and confirmation by his team that he was exercising regularly during his campaign for US presidency. If the candidate for the Oval Office can find time to exercise then you can too.

Exercise is indeed one of the habits shared by many of the world's most successful people, whether in business, finance, politics or academia. Most outperformers have long ago realised that instead of using alcohol, inappropriate behaviour, bad foods and drugs to release all the tension within one's body, good exercise is a much better way to relax.

Moreover, it has been proved scientifically that a healthier body – if doing regular, vigorous exercise – leads to an increased awareness of what is good for us. In particular, those who regularly exercise can tell much more quickly if they are doing something that is causing physical damage to their body. Such a person can tell when they are eating food that is damaging. Excessive alcohol has more of a negative effect on them. Staying up late at night feels more of a burden.

Exercise creates a belief in us – if done regularly – that a healthy body, as opposed to an unhealthy one, leads to happiness. It has been shown again and again that regular, rigorous exercise increases the endorphins and creates a stable, longer-term feeling of happiness.[84] When one really understands this connection then this will, over time, change the message that is being sent to our brain about how the body should be treated.

Last but not least, exercise also creates physical intelligence:[85] the ability to better communicate with our bodies when interacting with others.[86] Sports that are demanding in terms of body coordination make us feel more confident about the way we control our body. When we become more confident in terms of our body expressions, this has a tremendous positive effect on our charisma.

Perhaps the most powerful exercise in this sense is actually dancing, since in addition to requiring high body coordination it also requires a lot of confidence. When practised regularly, it becomes self-perpetuating and actually creates a high level of physical confidence.[87]

We have now given you evidence to convince your left brain about the benefits of exercise for your long-term success and happiness. The key to developing a healthy exercise habit is largely the same as with any other habit. The specific factors that seem to make the biggest difference in the likelihood of sticking to one's exercise habit are the following:

Firstly, make it as easy as possible to exercise. Find a gym that is as close to your school, office or home as possible. Prepare your kit the evening before. Reduce or avoid any distractions or obstacles that could give you a reason to skip exercise on a given day. If you plan to go to the gym after school or work, grab your stuff and go immediately after coming home – do not check your e-mails or what is on TV first.

Secondly, choose the right combination of exercise, and do not overdo it. Consult specialist literature, websites or your gym staff to set up the appropriate routine. Definitely go for cardio (running, cycling, swimming etc.) as opposed to weight training at the beginning, and always make sure that you have a large component of cardio in your schedule. The reason for this is that it is vigorous, cardio exercise that leads to the biggest build up in energy levels.

Thirdly, make your exercise schedule enjoyable, and ideally get your friends involved too. It can be both fun and worthwhile, at the beginning of a transition from no exercise to a peak of physical fitness, to start doing some form of group activity. This can be taking fitness classes or a game that requires all players to be present like football, hockey, basketball etc.

This a great way of sharing responsibility because not only do you have to be responsible to your own loving intent for fitness but also to everyone else who expects you to turn up. Especially at a competitive level (i.e. a league or cup), group sports make it much more difficult to skip a session as others rely on you.

One last comment on exercise and diet – make sure that you are very well hydrated, and not in caloric deficit immediately before, during and after exercise. Drink plenty of water and eat something light (ideally high in carbohydrates and protein) a couple of hours before. This is to make sure that you have enough energy to fuel your body while you exercise and for recovery and growth afterwards. Exercise on low energy is dangerous as it makes it easier for you to get injured.

Key Takeaways: Health and Fitness

- Of all the accounts, the physical account is the most capable of initiating both virtuous cycles and vicious circles. It can unleash a ferocious spiral in either direction. The outperformer is aware of this, and proactively makes use of it.

- Common sense is the best guide for your diet. Eat real food. Drink plenty of fluids, mostly water. Eat your meals in a way that mirrors your energy needs – more in the morning, less late at night. Do not be afraid to experiment. Do not disregard your body as a partner in terms of the feedback it gives you.

- Sleep is the single most efficient way of revitalising body and mind; do not regard it as an enemy to be fought against. Focus on the quality rather than quantity of your sleep. Experiment.

- Exercise is not an area of sacrifice and punishment. Make it highly enjoyable in order to develop a positive, sustainable habit.

Don't forget the previous chapter: Doing What You Love

- There is a difference between enjoying an activity because it is in your comfort zone and genuinely deriving pleasure from it.

- The outperformer understands this difference and its long-run impact on his or her life. It pays to focus your attention on making this distinction early, and changing your habits accordingly.

- Sustaining your enthusiasm is something which you can significantly influence using a few simple to use strategies. This is what outperformers across disciplines and across the world do.

- It is much easier for your brain to be motivated if the eventual goal is tangible, and if it impacts your senses. Translate your abstract goals into related visual images, smells, sounds, think about them often, and make it clear to your brain in this way that they are important.

Chapter 11

Communication

"Great minds discuss ideas; Average minds discuss events; Small minds discuss people."

Eleanor Roosevelt, First Lady of the United States

"The single biggest problem in communication is the illusion that it has taken place."

George Bernard Shaw, playwright

11.1 Open and honest communication

It is nothing short of shocking to realise how many problems and conflicts can be avoided and how many relationships can be improved when you set some simple rules of behaviour to ensure healthy relationships.

The first one is open and honest communication. Say honestly how you feel. A lot of the time, especially in the workplace, people start out either being too friendly or being too reserved. Both of these can give the wrong impression. If you are too reserved, colleagues will find it harder to act towards you with kindness, affection etc. and you will feel lonely. If you behave in a way that is too friendly and do not have boundaries then you can end up being hurt and overreacting towards someone and/or perceived to not take work seriously enough. Often a confused colleague will then say "You had no problems with that joke two days ago, why do you today?"

This confusion tends to be most prevalent in the interaction between the sexes – in the workplace, and sometimes at school. We are not talking about romantic relationships here, but about collegial or professional relationships. The reason why these relationships are particularly exposed to problems in communication is that men and women work on 'different communication protocols'. It is therefore vital that you are open and transparent as otherwise misunderstandings occur and both parties end up feeling insulted or ignored.

Another reason that it is so important to set the rules early is that often one person does not understand why the other person is unhappy. The most stereotypical example of this is the dialogue between a man and a woman when he asks "What is happening?" and she responds "Nothing" when obviously "a great deal" is the real answer.

There is generally a different perspective that women and men bring to the interaction and the only way to have a consistent relationship is to try and be as open and honest about your dialogue as you can. If you are not, you will create problems. And the most important rule to set at the beginning is the rule of open and transparent communication between the two individuals. This applies to professional relationships, friendships and romantic relationships alike.

When we are open and honest about how we feel and we do not try to pretend somehow that we are more thick-skinned then we are, then we really allow people to see us as we are.

We know that this is difficult and can be scary but the payoffs make it a worthwhile goal to aim for. The more you behave as you truly are, the more people can respond to the real you. The more they respond in this way, the more affection, the more real consideration and kindness there will be in the workplace. Because you will be consistently dealt with according to your temperament, you will feel more relaxed and natural.

11.2 Balancing anger and appreciation

It is one of the hardest things in life to look at the good things someone has done when you are angry with that person, and the other way round, actually (that 'honeymoon' period). Overlooking someone else's bad qualities for too long can ultimately lead to overreaction when you do wake up to it.

This is why it is so important, in any balanced relationship, romantic or otherwise, to constantly be aware that every person is going to have some good and some bad points. Similarly, you must be aware that in the beginning of every relationship you are likely to see the good points and towards the end of that relationship you will see the bad.

It is important that you create a balanced response at the beginning so that you are not too polite and consciously avoiding getting to see the truth about the other person. Similarly, do not be less critical later in the relationship just because you think 'Well that was always there so I am not going to be that critical of it'. If you manage to answer both issues, then that balance in the individual will lead to a sustainably loving relationship. It will be balanced in terms of your responses, regardless of the stage or the intensity of the relationship.

11.3 Consistency

Consistency in communication with both yourself and others is the key to emotional stability. Emotional stability happens when there is trust and dialogue between the four parts of the brain. It is consistency in our behaviour towards self and others that create this trust, and the brain to accept inputs from each of its four individual parts when interacting with others. This, in turn, leads to balance and stability in relationships.

More importantly, this also leads to stability and balance within ourselves. Consistency over time will lead to emotional stability, maturity and trust in oneself. Emotional fluctuation must then be an internal process; it is the indiscipline of the mind which leads to self attack or cruelty towards others.

This becomes even more important when you are in a place of leadership, as inevitably situations occur when some form of punishment is required – whether towards a junior employee, a member of a team of which you are a captain, or towards other children if you are a school prefect.

Here, the intent is very important. If the intent is that the punishment should be a corrective measure leading to an improvement of the individual rather than a way to vent one's own emotional frustration then you will be coming from a place of love. However, if you are just looking to feel better at the expense of the so-called 'weaker' individual then it is just plain cruelty.

Finally, consistency is also important across different parts of our lives, not just over time. We often apply different values when interacting with family, friends, colleagues and the society at large. What happens then is that this creates inconsistency and disconnect in your life which eventually demonstrates itself through pain and suffering.

Accepting these values as your core principles and behaving accordingly is one of the things that create great charisma. People who hold decent values unequivocally consistently convey attractiveness to others who hold similar values. In fact, the consistency of your values often increases your charisma even with people who do not share those values. It is important to expect and demand the same level of maturity when choosing and interacting with your friends.

Consistency must happen regardless of your immediate emotional state. Did someone at work behave in a way that caused you hurt, anxiety or discomfort? If you respond from the emotional state in which the hurt has been delivered, there will be a tendency to over-react towards the other person. The key quality of great leaders is to take a step back and try to focus at that moment on other things that are going well in your life. This improved and stabilizes your emotional state, allowing you to respond in the most appropriate way. This is the same principle as counting to 10, just a lot more efficient.

What happens if you stop using these or similar rules? You create, either with other individuals or within yourself, a discord and a cut-off which will stop them acting from a place of loyalty and affection. If you do not practise these rules on yourself, it will lead to disconnect from your inspiration.

Key Takeaways: Communication

- Being able to speak, listen, read and write does not in itself make a good communicator. A few simple rules can prevent misunderstandings and avoid unnecessary conflicts, yet not many people follow them. We offer the following three suggestions.

- Be honest and open about what you want to say, and how you feel. It allows people to see you as you really are, and react accordingly. Language is not absolute, and problems easily arise, especially with people from different backgrounds, cultures or professions. (And of the opposite sex!)

- Learn to balance anger and appreciation. Consciously start focusing on the good things someone has done when you are angry with that person, and the other way round (that 'honeymoon' period).

- Be consistent. Consistency leads to emotional stability in your relationships with others, as well as in your relationship with yourself. Consistency makes people trust you, and creates charisma.

Don't forget the previous chapter: Health and Fitness

- Of all the accounts, the physical account is the most capable of initiating both virtuous cycles and vicious circles. It can unleash a ferocious spiral in either direction. The outperformer is aware of this, and proactively makes use of it.

- Common sense is the best guide for your diet. Eat real food. Drink plenty of fluids, mostly water. Eat your meals in a way that mirrors your energy needs – more in the morning, less late at night. Do not be afraid to experiment. Do not disregard your body as a partner in terms of the feedback it gives you.

- Sleep is the single most efficient way of revitalising body and mind; do not regard it as an enemy to be fought against. Focus on the quality rather than quantity of your sleep. Experiment.

- Exercise is not an area of sacrifice and punishment. Make it highly enjoyable in order to develop a positive, sustainable habit.

Chapter 12
Relationships and Networking

"More business decisions occur over lunch and dinner than at any other time, yet no MBA courses are given on the subject."

Peter Drucker, consultant

"Be careful the environment you choose for it will shape you; be careful the friends you choose for you will become like them."

W. Clement Stone, businessman and philanthropist

12.1 Why do most people despise networking, and what can we do about it?

Advancements in communications continue to bring us closer to each other: the internet, mobile phones, satellite networks, low-cost airlines and so on. One of the remarkable consequences of these trends is that the decreasing distances have increased the importance of one's reputation and dependence on 'networks'.

Networks and relationships have always played a key role in business; recently, however, the two have become equally important in academia, science and research. Joint papers are a good indicator of this: in the 1960s, economists rarely produced joint work (just 12 percent of published articles in the top economics journals had two authors), but by the end of the 1990s joint work had become more common than not.[88]

This trend is very likely to continue and accelerate further, so contacts and networks are, and will be, crucially important to the outperformer of tomorrow. Unfortunately, networking is a concept that is often misunderstood, and this misunderstanding then creates a negative emotional response that can be detrimental to your performance, and life experience at large.

When I [Jan] first came to the UK and heard about networking, I took a strong and immediate dislike in the concept. Making an effort to meet new people just for the sake of taking advantage of their position, skills, connections, expertise, wealth etc. later seemed like the exact opposite of everything I had ever believed in. Over the next few years, I would gradually accept the concept. Partially, it was a function of those I held in great respect implicitly endorsing the practice, either by talking about it or doing it themselves. The epiphany moment, however, came when I realised that the common definition only applied to common networking – which, in most cases, does not really work. I thought there had to be a better way.

Even now, 5 years later, the expression itself – 'networking' – still produces the same kind of negative emotional response, and it takes my left brain a good deal of conscious effort to over-write these tendencies and convince my right brain that actually, there is nothing inherently wrong with the concept. And I do not seem to be the only one. Most people instinctively feel a negative emotion towards networking as a concept. When we hear that someone is an 'excellent networker', we often oscillate between positive and negative emotions with a bias towards the latter.

Why do networking and networkers produce such negative, or at best mixed, emotions and feelings? One of the key reasons is the diversity of activities and people commonly included under these expressions.

It is relatively easy to define what constitutes 'bad' networking. 'Networking events' with people standing around with drinks, exchanging business cards without even introducing themselves properly, pretentious behaviour, breaking conversations after two minutes to jump onto the next person, having no real interest in the other individual and what they have to say (yet adding them as a LinkedIn/Facebook friend afterwards for the sake of it), pointless, shallow conversations, lots of talking about self and not listening, gossip, sleazy salesmen types everywhere around. This will sound very familiar to some of you; the rest have not missed out on anything.

These are the characteristics of bad networking, and bad networkers. As it turns out, defining 'good' networking is a lot more difficult. If you define networking in the conventional sense as **the process of meeting new people in order to build mutually beneficial relationships**, it is insufficient. It lacks specificity in its description of both the interaction and the purpose. When does networking stop being networking and turns into friendships, or partnerships? All of our relationships should be mutually beneficial, not just those we classify as 'networking'.

"Expose yourself to as much randomness as possible" is a quote from *My Start-Up Life*[89], a book by Ben Casnocha. Ben is an entrepreneur and a successful blogger; he is 21 years old and serves on the board of Comcate, Inc., the leading e-government technology firm he founded eight years ago. In this context, the value of the quote above comes from just how well it summarizes what networking is really about.

Think about your best friends. How did you meet them? The odds are, at least a few of them just happened to be in the same class, school, sports team or college choir. Even more 'worryingly', some of them just happened to be at the same birthday or dinner party, on the same trip or perhaps expedition. But then, what if you did not happen to be in that same class, school, sports team, on that same trip?

Would your life be less interesting? Would you still have such great friends? And conversely, what if you could have gone to more classes, schools, or trips? Would you have more 'best friends', or 'better best friends'? What about your wider network of cool acquaintances? Most people seem to find their 'best friends' even if they only attend one school. But some do not. Most people are happy about their 'best friends'. But some are not.

As Keith Ferrazzi, author of *Never Eat Alone*[90] and one of the most connected people in the world according to *Forbes* magazine once said: *"networking is about inviting others into your life"*. That is a fundamental difference – inviting others into your life, rather than pushing yourself into theirs, is a huge difference in mindsets and attitudes.

This is why Ben's quote clicked with me when I first read it, and has remained one of my favourites ever since. Today, I believe that one of its best application is to people and relationships, and hence to networking. "Expose yourself to randomness", when applied to meeting people, forms the basis of my definition of true networking. I believe that networking is about putting yourself into situations where you are likely to meet people you would not meet otherwise, or who you would not normally get to know at all. Networking is about going out there, finding out more about others and telling them a bit about you. It is nothing more than that.

I hate the idea of going to strangers to effectively say "Hi, this is me and this is why you better become friends with me". I quite like the idea of going to strangers to say "Hi, this is me and these are the things I am passionate about. If we have something in common, great, if not, it was nice to meet you". This distinction – while subtle – makes all the difference.

There is one other important difference between how most people define and see networking, and the approach of those who really make it work. The usual definitions of networking are not just about meeting people and the initial contact; they also talk about how to build a mutually beneficial relationship, help others, reach out, and harness the fruits of your effort. This is a related, but fundamentally really quite different concept.

Networking is what we described above. The rest – being a likeable person, having good manners, being always willing to help and build mutually beneficial relationships – is, or should be, nothing more than common sense that applies to all of our relationships.

12.2 How to become better with people

Better people skills are easy to identify, but really tough to implement. These are the tricks of the trade that get you furthest the quickest:

Say hello and smile[91]

This is one of those ridiculously simple things that everyone knows, but for some reason most of us forget to do it every day.

Just walk through the streets of your town or city, or in fact through the corridors at schools, university or in the office, and try to count the number of people who smile, or say hi. If you feel that this number is sufficiently high, then you are either lucky about where you live, study or work, or have very low expectations. For most of us, the experience is unfortunately likely to be quite depressing.

Now try another example. Walk through the same streets and corridors and smile at random people or say hi to those you know only vaguely, the kind of people you keep seeing around but never talk to them. Count how many people smile back. The large majority of those who notice you will smile back or say "hi" too. People follow very simple behavioural patterns in certain areas, and this is one of them. If someone smiles at you, you will smile back without even thinking about it. For some reason, this decision happens on a subconscious level for most people.

> *"When you smile, I smile, that's the deal.*
>
> *I will not walk past you and not look you in the eyes and not acknowledge you.*
>
> *Instead we will pass each other and say hello – not with our words, for they are not the same, but with our faces.*
>
> *I meet you, and I see there is good in your eyes; there's passion in your heart; and there's a friendly hello in your smile; and for the first time we can relate and appreciate each other.*
>
> *It is all it takes.*
>
> *It is where it starts.*
>
> *Because I know that you will smile, and I will smile, and all the rest is easy."*
>
> *Celebrate Humanity* advert, Sydney Summer Olympics, 2000

Drop your story

One of the greatest inertia in us is our 'story', or what we believe ourselves to be. Depending on the background you have been brought up in, certain beliefs about the world, the way society works, fairness, equity, equality etc. will have been formed in your mind. These will have created the basis of your behavioural patterns. Hence, some people expect to be helped by everyone around them, while others are shy to ask even their best friends for help.

Your story is often your biggest obstacle when you try to connect with other people. Effective communicators master their story and make it just that – a story. They change their perspective and stop being influenced by the 'noise' of their past. Great leaders cleanse their stories so that their intuition and inspiration are not coloured by trauma or fear, or conversely hubris and pride.

Know your own trigger points and control them. The greatest part of your story, or perspective, is created during childhood. Both pride and insecurity not only drain you emotionally, they also make connecting with people more difficult. Disregard your story to make interactions with others for a common goal easier. The United States has taken this to the extreme – its story as a nation takes a back seat to the goal of material enrichment.

Constantly revise your mental map of the world, for not only does our motivation evolve from our perspective, but the way we interact with other people depends upon it. What we want and expect of other people and the way we behave towards them, all tend to be determined by our earlier experience.

If you spent much of your childhood helping out your friends at school, and they always disappointed you and misused your help and trust, you are likely to reflect this story in your behaviour today, even if the people you interact with today deserve trust and help. The converse also applies.

Learn how to get others to drop their barriers

We naturally have certain barriers when interacting with other people. These work intuitively – when you say bye to your parents and get in the car with your friends, the framework of your behaviour changes. Similarly, when your teacher stops you halfway through your discussion with a friend, you immediately adopt a different attitude, posture, language etc., before you respond to the teacher.

This is even more pronounced when we interact with new people or people we don't know well. The challenge for anyone looking to connect with others quickly is to make the other person drop their barriers more quickly than usual. This applies across different people and relationship, regardless of whether you are looking to become friends, create a good collegial working relationship or get the other person to buy something from you.

Think about your best friends and how long it took before your friendship got to a point where you would comfortably discuss things that are normally considered quite personal – emotional and romantic relationships, life ambitions and dreams, childhood experiences, family facts and stories.

People who are excellent networkers, communicators and persuaders have the ability to make you drop those barriers much quicker. You may have experienced this before when you met someone and within hours you were discussing the sort of things listed above. We usually say that we 'clicked' with the other person in such situations. The best communicators know how to significantly increase the chances of 'clicking' with other people.

There are different ways of getting others to drop their barriers. The first step is to learn how to control your own story as previously explained. If you drop your own story, and hence your barriers, there is one 'wall' to climb over instead of two. There are two key strategies that make people drop their barriers.

Find what you have in common with the other person and temporarily become more like them in certain aspects. Simple techniques that you can use and experiment with include adopting the same posture as the other person (sensibly!) and synchronising your body language, using the other person's gestures and tone of voice, being generally positive and asking many open ended questions. Practise smiling during conversations with your friends so that it comes naturally when conversing with strangers.

Language is important too. Not only does it help to use some of the other person's words, it is often also useful to determine how they think and prefer to receive information – are they visual, auditory or kinaesthetic? Phrases and words they use such as "I see", "I hear what you're saying", "I know where you're coming from" are dead giveaways as to how your sparring partner thinks. If you tend to use "I hear what you're saying" more often than other phrases, it is likely that you also prefer using "This does not sound right" rather than "That does not strike me as right". Learn how to identify how others think, and adjust your language accordingly.

Experiment and evaluate

Experimentation is generally underrated when it comes to personal development. While some of the advice we can offer is applicable across different environments and for different people, there will inevitably be some things that only work for you, because of who you are and what environment you live in.

What we can recommend, however, is to experiment with different strategies, and then evaluate them retrospectively. This may sound way over the top at first, but tackling relationships and networking in the same way that an athlete tackles a certain discipline has been widely acknowledged as one of the best strategies used by the world's leading experts on the subject.[92]

All this requires is a conscious decision to try out different things, and then have the discipline to come back to them and identify what worked, and what did not.

Fake it until you make it

We find it difficult to change, especially when it comes to changing the way we portray ourselves to others. It is extremely hard to suddenly become more confident when dealing with others, or to become the one taking the initiative, or to open up and share more about ourselves etc.

One of the best ways of overcoming this natural resistance is to trick the mind by playing a game. More specifically, if you wish to become X, play a game with your mind and behave as if you were X. Pretend for a day that you are X. What would you do differently? How would you feel about yourself? This sounds, like many great ideas, way too simple to work but has been proved again and again to be extremely helpful.

Do you want to become more outgoing? Behave as if you were. Force yourself to step into your new character and meet a new person every day, start a conversation with the shop assistant or restaurant staff, ask for directions etc. Step by step, you will change from who you are to the person you have been acting like. If you need a further boost, change your physical image too – a new 'confident' hairstyle, item of clothing, pair of shoes or watch can make a huge difference in helping you change your personality. Finally, change your environment to make it even easier. Are you afraid to behave like this with people you know? Start with complete strangers. Go to places you do not normally visit and practise there.

Work on the most important components of your charisma.

Personal charisma is normally seen as something intangible that just happens. But actually, we can de-construct what creates charisma. The two most important factors are your speaking style, including voice, tone, language and delivery, and your body language and gesticulation, including body confidence.

There are a number of activities that can help you improve your speaking style. Basically, you need to find activities that will put you in a position where you need to frequently communicate with and convince a large number of other people, often at the same time, or alternatively that put you in frequent contact with very senior people. These can include roles in various societies and organisations, or certain hobbies, such as debating or public speaking clubs.

We have already mentioned one of the best ways of improving your body confidence – sports that include difficult body coordination, and dancing in particular. Becoming involved in these or other similar activities that involve the same requirements and challenges should over time help you become aware of your body language. You will then progressively learn to control it, both consciously and subconsciously.

There are then clearly a number of other things that play a part in creating charisma. These are often quite simple, e.g. always remembering everyone's names and details they share with you, or common beliefs and values, as we already explained in the chapter on Responsibility. The best way to develop these skills further is by experimenting and evaluating what works, or alternatively studying more specialised literature on the subject which can also provide specific exercises and tips for adopting these new habits.

Be open about your interests, passions and dedication

Most of us feel quite comfortable discussing intimate details of our romantic lives with those we trust, yet relatively few people feel comfortable talking with complete honesty about their interests and passions. For some reason, we feel that we must be cautious, and hide the most extreme visions and dreams from others.

Understand the power of being open about your passions and what you want from life, and make use of it. When others see that you are passionate and dedicated to something, they will tend to assume that you are going to succeed in pursuing your dreams which makes them much more inclined to help you as they will not see their effort as wasted, and they will believe that whatever help they offer will be useful and create goodwill.

It is particularly important to engender this goodwill when dealing with people more senior than you whether they are teachers, professors or managers. There are very few things that you can offer to someone who is much more senior than you are, but passion, dedication and commitment to a common cause go a long way.

Thousands of books have been written by people who are experts in being great communicators, and if you are particularly interested in this area, we would encourage you to go and explore it further. Having said that, you can reap much of the low hanging fruit by implementing the concepts outlined above well.

12.3 How to build winning relationships

Building successful relationships is about figuring out what you want, what the other party wants, and finding the best way of meeting both parties' needs. What does 'best way' mean? Sometimes those interests are too divergent, and 'best way' means never interacting again or perhaps becoming loose business acquaintances. Other times, it may mean becoming friends, starting a business together or even marrying each other and living happily ever after.

There is a natural spectrum of acceptance of another human being. At the low end there is complete rejection, at the other, unconditional love. Building a successful relationship is all about moving a given relationship to a place where both parties like it to be on their spectrum of acceptance.

1. Understand what both parties want, and deliver it

The ability to understand what it is that both parties want from the relationship and to find the optimal balance between their needs (across their accounts) is at the very core of building successful relationships.

2. Learn how to like people and not envy them

These are two fundamental prerequisites for being able to build winning relationships. Sadly, most people have a problem with one or the other condition to some degree. We will therefore look briefly at both problems now, and try to identify what goes wrong in both cases.

There are those who say that they just do not like other people. This statement is misleading, for it makes no distinction between liking other people and liking interaction with other people. The two are fundamentally different. Each of us is different, and has a different degree of necessity or desire to spend time interacting with others. This is absolutely natural.

There is, however, nothing natural about not liking other people per se. A sizeable proportion of the world's population would unfortunately classify themselves as falling under this category. There are a number of reasons for why they believe this to be the case. In reality, the sad truth is that if you do not like other people as such, there is something dysfunctional in your way of thinking. In the long-term, such a stance is beneficial neither to you nor to society at large. If you therefore feel that you fit this description to some degree, you definitely need to re-examine your values and thinking, and identify the cause of this dysfunctionality.

Envy is even more prevalent; indeed, very few people in the world could claim to have entirely mastered this emotion. For obvious reasons, envy is one of major obstacles in building successful relationships. Identifying if and when you feel this way, and reversing this emotion is therefore a necessary prerequisite for creating the way of thinking that is helpful to building winning relationships.

3. Create goodwill and help others succeed

We said earlier that the key is to understand what the other party wants and help them achieve this. The key to successful and **leveraged** relationships is therefore to do this as much as possible. The ideal win-win scenario that leads to winning relationships is therefore when both parties can do things that do not mean much to us but mean a lot to the other person, and expect the same way the other way round. This creates an enormous amount of goodwill on both parts of the relationship.

4. Go for quality, not quantity and always be genuine

We explained earlier what constitutes 'bad' networking, and this point builds on the spirit of that. Compromising on who you are, what you want, who the other person is and what they want and can offer in order to increase the number of relationships you can have is a sure way to unhappiness and underperformance. Sadly, this is something that many do on a habitual basis.

Always being 100% genuine is the best way to avoid entering or staying in relationships that involve pretence, or compromising your needs and wants. It also naturally leads to a smaller number of high quality relationships as opposed to a large number of lower quality ones.

It is important to understand that means of expression is different from content. Your content must always stay

genuine but if the other person is, for example, blind or deaf, you need to communicate by the appropriate medium.

While there are certain fields where one needs a large number of relationships that can be based on low interaction (politics, for example), this should never mean that we compromise on their quality. To put it differently, the most respected politicians tend to be those who remain consistent about who they are and what their vision is, as opposed to those that tailor and twist their story in order to please others.

Key Takeaways: Relationships and Networking

- Do not let your romantic relationships and friendships lead to underperformance. Develop a healthy perspective on relationships, and create an expectation of only being in those relationships that are healthy.

- Healthy relationships are based on a consistent, rational interaction that leads to an increase in the Four Accounts, and that works in a kind, considerate and affectionate way.

- We live in an increasingly inter-connected world and so networking is a key skill for the outperformer. The term is often misunderstood today, and that is why it can have negative connotations.

- 'Good' networking is about inviting others into your life. 'Bad' networking is about pushing yourself into theirs. People who actually make networking work understand this, and adopt a healty approach to networking.

- Becoming better with people and building winning relationships can be summarised in two points – smile, and understand what both parties want from the interaction.

Don't forget the previous chapter: Communication

- Being able to speak, listen, read and write does not in itself make a good communicator. A few simple rules can prevent misunderstandings and avoid unnecessary conflicts, yet not many people follow them. We offer the following three suggestions.

- Be honest and open about what you want to say, and how you feel. It allows people to see you as you really are, and react accordingly. Language is not absolute, and problems easily arise, especially with people from different backgrounds, cultures or professions. (And of the opposite sex!)

- Learn to balance anger and appreciation. Consciously start focusing on the good things someone has done when you are angry with that person, and the other way round (that 'honeymoon' period).

- Be consistent. Consistency leads to emotional stability in your relationships with others, as well as in your relationship with yourself. Consistency makes people trust you, and creates charisma.

Chapter 13
Mentors and Buddies

"Young men think old men are fools; but old men know young men are fools."

George Chapman, dramatist and poet

"Children are always the only future the human race has; teach them well."

Unknown

13.1   Why are mentors and buddies important?

Mentoring and buddy systems have been adopted by leading companies, from technology giants to investment banks, all over the world. In most cases, these programmes even have the same or very similar structure. Why? They work, and immediately add real, tangible value.

If you ask many of the world's most successful people about what helped them get where they are today, you are likely to receive a wide range of very different answers. One of the few things that will almost always be present on their lists, regardless of whether you talk to athletes, musicians, entrepreneurs, politicians, bankers, academics or members of any other profession, is that they all had great mentors, and committed buddies or colleagues.

A mentoring relationship takes place between two individuals and usually revolves around some shared area of interest, even if it is as vague as 'business' or 'arts'. There is typically a significant difference in seniority between them in this area. While it tends to be the case that the mentor is naturally much older than the mentee, this is by no means universal – someone switching careers might well end up being mentored by someone younger. The relationship is based on a mutual understanding that the mentor is committed to helping the mentee develop and improve by passing on his accumulated experience and expertise.

A buddy relationship is similar to a mentoring one, except that the two individuals are typically of roughly similar seniority. The relationship is then based on a mutual commitment to helping each other succeed in whatever is the focus of the relationship – typically a sports or academic goal, professional development, learning some skill etc.

Investment banks and financial services companies in general are some of the most passionate proponents of this system, having successfully practised it for many years. At most firms, a junior employee is assigned at least one mentor and one buddy often even before joining the firm, and quickly becomes engaged in bringing up the next generation only a couple of years later. Many firms have adopted similar practices because these systems are the most efficient way of spreading accumulated knowledge within the company and passing it on to the next generation of leaders. The same buddy and mentoring relationships exist in the world of entrepreneurship, albeit in a less formal way. For obvious reasons, they tend to be initiated directly by the parties involved rather than planned by the firm.

These systems are very efficient because both you and your mentor/buddy are committed to practising a mutually nurturing relationship. As your subconscious starts feeling the benefits of this behaviour, it will hopefully start copying that mode of behaviour in all relationships. Mentoring and buddy systems provide a blueprint of mutual commitment to personal growth for all your other relationships making them a powerful and efficient tool to leverage your new-found skills.

13.2   How to find great buddies

The primary consideration when finding a buddy has to be to do with their skill set. As we explained earlier, building winning relationships is about understanding what both parties want from the interaction, and meeting those needs. Ideally, you should therefore first establish what you want from your buddy. Do you need motivational support? Do you need someone to look out for you and help you with any problems you encounter? Do you need someone who has a different skill set and can help you improve in certain areas? You should also consider what you can offer the other person.

These are the primary questions you need to ask yourself. Next is compatibility. The relationship between buddies is one of equals, so it is important to find someone who has not only a shared goal with you but who is similarly likely to achieve that goal. The buddy should be on a similar level in terms of their professional and emotional growth and development. More importantly, their desire to succeed should be even greater than your own thus inspiring you to future outperformance.

Buddy relationships work best when both parties achieve similar levels of progress and success. Working together with someone who would otherwise be seen as a competitor is quite difficult. We talked about envy and how to tackle it in the previous chapter, but that does not mean that one can assume it will not happen in their relationships; it is important to stay very vigilant about this.

Uneven achievements tend to create resentment at best and envy at worst on one side while creating a feeling of pulling the other person's weight on the other. Mutual compatibility is therefore of utmost importance in a buddy relationship – are you starting from similar positions, with similar potential and a shared ambition? Are you both really committed to helping each other, and able to see the rest of the world, but not each other, as competition?

Once you have identified suitable friends, classmates or colleagues, there is of course a certain amount of emotional intelligence needed when deciding on how to approach the other person with your suggestion. Being completely open and honest about what you are trying to achieve, what you are offering and using the advice from previous chapters should help you to convince the other person of the benefits of your proposal.

13.3 How to find great mentors

Mentors, by definition, come from a broader range of fields than buddies. Most people who have achieved a certain level of success and accumulated a certain amount of experience in any given area will have something to teach you. It may be very directly connected to your areas of interest, or it may be something as vague as 'life advice'.

Similarly to the dilemmas you face when looking for buddies, it makes sense to really think about where you see your biggest opportunities for personal development, and then find a mentor who can guide and support you in those areas. This has indeed been the case with the authors of this book. The mentor-mentee partnership between Muzaffar and Jan has been hugely beneficial to both parties; while we share certain interests, such as financial markets, we have fundamentally different personalities and come from practically opposite backgrounds.

On the other hand, there is also an argument to be made for looking for exceptional people first, and turning your relationship with them into a mentoring one second. Anyone truly exceptional will have something very valuable to teach you, and in our experience it is often those relationships, where the link is not immediately obvious, that end up making the biggest difference.

The other important consideration is, of course, whether the potential mentor is someone who has an interest in mentoring others. While this can be difficult to judge initially and it is not something you can ask about directly, spending more time with this person should soon give you a good idea.

Converting potential mentors into real mentors can be quite difficult, especially if you aim very high. There are a couple of things that can significantly increase your chances. Firstly, very senior people respond extremely well to passion, commitment and dedication. The people who make it to the top are by default mostly those who exhibited these qualities in their early years. Seeing someone young being passionate about their field of interest is like seeing themselves many years earlier and this creates a natural connection.

Secondly, do not approach senior people asking them to become your mentors straight away; this approach rarely works and does not project the best image of you as a potential mentee. The best mentoring relationships develop naturally over time, step by step. Try to spend more time with the person. Ask good questions. If you can, add value to them as well – there are certain topics where even someone much younger can provide significant value to a very senior individual. These can include doing research or other specific tasks that are necessary but mundane.

Over time, if you act with honesty and integrity, and demonstrate passion and dedication, people who make good mentors will start taking a natural interest in you, and the relationship will develop from there.

On a final note, it is important that you understand the different roles that buddies and mentors play in the outperformer's life. While there will inevitably be some overlap, it helps if you approach these relationships with a good deal of rationality and structure. Once you establish your buddy or mentor relationships, do not be afraid to be very specific about what you want to achieve, and what you can offer. The other party will almost always appreciate and reciprocate your efforts.

Key Takeaways: Mentors and Buddies

- Many successful people attribute their achievements to the help they have received from their mentors and buddies. These relationships provide an opportunity to learn from others and accelerate your own development.

- Find good buddies who will support you in your goals and vision. Focus on identifying people who are compatible – they should be on a similar level of achievement and motivation, and have complementary skills to your own.

- There are two approaches to finding mentors. Identify the areas where you want to work on yourself, and find people with the right experience and skills. Alternatively, find people who are just amazing, and go for it with the understanding that there is bound to be something they tan teach you.

- Converting potential mentors into real mentors can be quite difficult, especially if you aim very high. The best strategy is to show your passion, commitment and dedication, and try to spend more time with the person.

Don't forget the previous chapter: Relationships and Networking

- Do not let your romantic relationships and friendships lead to underperformance. Develop a healthy perspective on relationships, and create an expectation of only being in those relationships that are healthy.

- Healthy relationships are based on a consistent, rational interaction that leads to an increase in the Four Accounts, and that works in a kind, considerate and affectionate way.

- We live in an increasingly inter-connected world and so networking is a key skill for the outperformer. The term is often misunderstood today, and that is why it can have negative connotations.

- 'Good' networking is about inviting others into your life. 'Bad' networking is about pushing yourself into theirs. People who actually make networking work understand this, and adopt a healthy approach to networking.

- Becoming better with people and building winning relationships can be summarised in two points – smile, and understand what both parties want from the interaction.

Chapter 14
Racing Against Time

"You may delay, but time will not."

Benjamin Franklin, Founding Father of the United States

"It is wonderful how much may be done if we are always doing."

Thomas Jefferson, 3rd President of the United States

14.1 Why time matters more than other things, and how to structure your time?

Time is the most precious resource we have as it can be exchanged readily for increases in our Four Accounts. "Do not waste time with unproductive activities, thoughts, relationships, objectives etc." has been the underlying theme but even so, it is beneficial to dedicate a chapter to habits that can help you become more efficient in some of the most time-demanding tasks faced by most if not all students and graduates during their studies, at work and in life in general.

This chapter will address one of the major issues – how should you divide your time between the different things you do? The next two chapters will then look at ways of saving time on those activities that tend to account for the biggest part of the normal day for students and junior professionals – work with computers, e-mail, typing, reading and memorising facts and numbers.

The tool we use to assess time allocation is a personal time matrix. The matrix has two forms. One is a grid consisting of 7 columns, representing week days, and 24 rows, representing hours in a day. The other is rectangle of the same size and shape where we group the blocks corresponding to time spent by activities, rather than by the time of the day and the day of the week when they take place_

> You can download both forms of the personal time matrix on our website, www.racing-towards-excellence.com.

The first function of the matrix is to tell you how much of your life is driven by habit and comfort zones and how much by the desire to improve, evolve and outperform. That gives you some idea of the journey that you have ahead. The knowledge of the length of that journey is a useful roadmap and a realistic calibrator of your short, medium and long-term expectations.

Secondly, by crystallising the opportunity cost of your activities, the matrix helps when making changes to your allocation of time. Once you know how much time you spend on different activities, you can figure out where time can be freed up, and where it is then best utilised in order to increase your Four Accounts.

How should you use the time matrix? Start by filling in the chronological version of the matrix for your typical week. Then add up your total amounts of time spent on each activity, and fill in a new matrix where blocks of time spent on the same activities are grouped together. Now you have a great overview of what you spend your time on every week.

Next, identify what activities are missing in your matrix – these will include both activities helping you achieve your goals and vision as well as positive leisure activities you would like to start doing. Allocate an appropriate amount of time to each of these activities.

Then look at your existing time matrix, and find activities that you can cut down on in order to free up the amount of time you need to introduce the new activities with the least damage to your performance and happiness. These should include pointless waste of time activities such as watching TV without any particular interest in the programme, wasting time on negative (gossipy, non-inspirational) social networks and using the internet unproductively and other similar things.

Then look at your existing matrix once again, and decide whether you can free up more time without compromising on your performance or happiness in a major way. If so, free it up and then think about what you could do in those hours.

Finally, once you have your new distribution of time between activities aggregated by those activities, start transferring this back into the original matrix type where activities correspond to days of the week and hours of the day. Give this some thought and find the most appropriate schedule that respects external constraints on what you need to do and when while at the same time being sensible about what activities are best done when.

For example, if you want to spend more time reading, you may want to schedule some free time after school so that you can use the library. Conversely, if you would like to schedule time for being with friends or talking to them online, it may make sense to put this into late evening hours when most people tend to be less productive anyway, so that you can make use of the morning and afternoon hours for things that are more mentally challenging, such as studies or work.

14.2   How to become more efficient with e-mail

The tool that was meant to simplify our lives and save our time has turned for many people into the ultimate productivity killer. At the extreme, Tim Ferris, the author of the bestselling *The Four Hour Workweek*, has developed a business that allows him to check his e-mails once a week, though most professionals can survive on checking their e-mail twice a day. But what if you are a news reporter, an investment banker or a secretary and have to have your Inbox switched on 100% of your time, thus being glued to your Blackberry or iPhone?

Some of the advice we give is generic and can be applied across careers and industries. Depending on your role, you may need to adapt some of it. Those of you still at school or university are somewhat fortunate in this matter as you should have sufficient freedom when it comes to e-mails.

Entire books and blogs have been written on e-mail processing and use and we absolutely recommend reading more on the subject if it is of interest. Following David Allen's

Getting Things Done[93] (GTD) philosophy however seems to stand at the basics of most systems used nowadays, and has been proved to work well for a wide range of individuals:

Start by creating a suitable folder structure, e.g. Work, School, Friends etc., with further subfolders (different school subjects in School, different activities/hobbies in Friends etc.) if needed. Then add the following three special folders: _1To-Do, _2Waiting-For, _3Maybe. The reason we use _ and numbers in front of the names is to make sure they rank right up below your Inbox at the top of the entire structure.

Once you have the structure in place, start checking your Inbox as infrequently as you can. For most students, once a day should be sufficient – if you have a very active online life, try twice a day.[94] When checking your e-mail, apply one of the following actions to every e-mail in your inbox –

    a. **Respond** – if it takes less than 2 minutes to respond to the e-mail, do so, whether this means taking an action, writing a reply or both.

    b. **Postpone** – if a response is needed, but it would take more than 2 minutes, move the e-mail into your _1To-Do folder.

    c. **Flag as maybe** – if the e-mail contains a request you do not have to respond to, but you would like if there is some time left, or if it is an article or a newsletter that you would like to read although it is not necessary, move the e-mail into your _3Maybe folder.

    d. **Archive** – if the e-mail is important and could be useful later, but does not require you to take any actions, move it to the appropriate folder.

    e. **Delete** – if the e-mail does not require an action and is unlikely to be important in the future, delete it.

Whenever you open your e-mail, you **must** process your entire Inbox all the way to **zero**. There should be no e-mails left in your Inbox when you finish – anything that requires your further attention should be in either _1To-Do or _3Maybe.

Depending on the urgency of the tasks you normally deal with, you can then create the appropriate routine for cleaning up the To-Do and Maybe folders. Generally speaking, people would normally process their To-Do folder at frequencies ranging between once a day to once a week. You should also clean your Maybe folder periodically, perhaps once every two to four weeks?

Finally, set your email client software to save sent e-mails into a 'Sent' or equivalent folder. Whenever you send an e-mail where the recipient's response is important to you, take that copy of your e-mail and move it from the Sent folder to your _2Waiting-For folder. You can then go through your Waiting-For folder every couple of days or so, and figure out if certain people are running behind schedule and/or if you need to send some reminders, call people up etc.

That wasn't a big deal, was it? For those of you dealing with limited number of e-mails, this may sound like a bit of an over-kill. The reason why we still recommend adapting this technique is that it creates good practice, and you will reap the rewards later on when your e-mail workload increases.

The system may sound a little bit too rule-based at first, but give it a go and see what you think in a month. Most people love it for one simple reason – like all good habits, it puts the decision making on auto-pilot and let's you get on with the work itself.

14.3 How to become more efficient with computers

The 80–20 rule is key to making time savings with comput-ers. The following few habits should help you improve your efficiency when using computers, if you have not adopted them yet. They sound simple, but do not underestimate the cumulative impact they can have.

Start with cleaning your desktop. *As I [Jan] am writing these lines, there are 5 icons on my desktop – My Computer, Firefox (internet browser), Thunderbird (e-mail client), Recycle Bin and a spreadsheet I use as an organiser. I can't see a reason why anyone would need to have more than 10 icons on their desktop.*

Having fewer icons helps for three key reasons: it makes your computer run quicker; it removes the mental clutter and forces you to organise your files properly; it makes it less likely that you will procrastinate by reducing the chances that you start looking through your songs, pictures, movies or playing your favourite game while switching between different windows.

Create a proper folder structure. There are managers who look at their interns' folder structure before making decisions on whether to hire them full-time or not. While it is possible to know where to find everything even if your hard drive is a mess, this will inevitably require mental attention and memory that could be better utilised elsewhere. Organising things properly creates clarity, allows you to focus on the important stuff and makes it less likely that you will lose or accidentally overwrite things.

If on Windows, get a proper file manager. This is software that allows you to browse the content of your hard drive(s). Most people use the default explorer – in our view, these are a drag on productivity and should be replaced immediately. Not all old things are bad – get something that resembles the way the old Norton Commander used to work under MS-DOS, such as TotalCmd, and save yourself a lot of hassle and time.

(We hear that the file manager on Mac is actually quite good; this rule applies predominantly to Windows where the consensus is clear and loud.)

Utilise the quick launch panel on Windows/Dock on Mac OS X. Quick Launch is the name of the small part of your taskbar (the – usually grey – thing at the side/bottom/top of your screen) next to the Start button. It usually contains a few icons, including Internet Explorer and Outlook. This is a great productivity tool. Place icons of software you use frequently onto the panel. This will save your nerves and time when you work.

Uninstall useless software. *I [Jan] probably rank about 8/10 on the computer geekiness scale. I still have fewer than 15 pieces of software installed on my laptop, with the large majority of these being small utility-style applications. Having tons of software you never use on your computer slows it down, and the cumulative effect can be shocking. Go through your installed programs, and uninstall each program you have not used in the last three months unless you see a specific reason to keep it.*

Back-up regularly. This is one of those pieces of advice that you hear all the time, and still will not follow. Then you lose the only copy of your dissertation a day before the deadline, spend your summer re-writing it and swear to back-up every other day for the rest of your life. Two years later, you realise that you latest back-up copy was taken six months ago. It *is* tedious. It is also unlikely that you will ever need to use your back-up copy. But the consequences can be disastrous.

To put it differently: the probability of this event happening is small, but the potential damage is huge. Remember how the Credit Crunch started? It was with a low-probability, practically impossible, event.

Get an additional monitor (or six of them). This one is for the more advanced users. You will not believe the difference this can make until you try it. So try it, or at least read about the experience of others who have. Google can provide you with a wealth of reviews and opinions. If you can afford it, give it some thought – the payoff is very tangible and very quick.

14.4 How to become more efficient with key skills

Governments all over the world have been changing our primary and secondary education by introducing a number of key skills into the curriculum – knowledge, application, analysis, evaluation etc. The problem is that they got it all wrong. The real key skills are much simpler than that and fundamentally comprise reading, touch-typing and memorisation.

We live in a world overwhelmed with information, with many suffering from information and news overload while struggling to keep up with the ever increasing expectations of school, university and the workplace on the amount of output we are expected to produce. Today's governments believe that children should be trained in analysing this information better, and on a theoretical level, such a strategy makes sense. The problem is that analysis is not something that can be easily taught, especially at primary or secondary school level.

Once again, there are much lower hanging fruit. What if you could read three and write three times as much in the same amount of time? Do you think you would be able to increase your productivity, produce better analysis and make better decisions? Absolutely. Having more information has proven the best way of making smarter choices across industries and academic disciplines. Learning how to touch-type and hence have the opportunity to communicate one's thoughts more fully and in greater detail in less time leads to better results, too.

So why do we stop training children to read very early on, and rarely teach them how to touch-type at all? Most of them will spend a significant proportion of their studies and careers typing. Notes, comments, reports, letters, e-mails, discussion board contributions, messages, text messages etc. Our very conservative estimate is that the average child born today in a developed country will type **135 million** characters in their lifetime.[95]

Similarly, facts and numbers and our ability to memorise them have become extremely important. Of course we have encyclopaedias and unlimited storage space on our computers, but what really limits our ability to make smart decisions and be productive in whatever we do is the constant need to look-up facts and numbers. Imagine the results you could achieve at school, university or work if you could remember a larger proportion of the facts you read every day. Important dates, equations, figures, profit numbers, margin estimates, telephone numbers, prices, exchange rates, statistics, research figures etc., the list goes on. So what are we going to do about it?

Firstly, how do you increase your reading speed? Reading is underrated as a skill. There are three major challenges involved in increasing our reading speed. Sub-vocalisation is the 'hearing of your voice' as you read. This is, in fact, the way you were taught to read – the teacher read words aloud to you, and you were then told to read them 'silently' to yourself. The problem is that while this technique is helpful at the beginning, it becomes a hindrance on our reading speed – we can see and comprehend text quicker than we can sub-vocalise it, so the latter becomes the limiting factor. Regression is the frequent re-reading of words that you have already seen. Lastly, mind drift stems from our ability to think much more quickly than we can read – the mind therefore drifts 'ahead' and we lose focus.

When a child starts learning how to read, she faces all three of these challenges, and reads at less than 100 words per minute. Very quickly, she will progress to read at 100 to 200 words per minute – this is a typical reading speed for children between 6 and 12 years old. This speed is also typical for an adult who has avoided reading for most of his life. Regression, sub-vocalisation and mind drift are all still very present.

Most people then progress into the 200–250 words per minute category – and get stuck there for the rest of their lives! This is the average reading speeding for the large majority of people. Although we generally conquer most problems with regression by then, sub-vocalisation is still present and we face occasional problems with mind drift. A minority push the bar a little bit higher, and read between 250 and 350 words per minute, mostly by reducing the degree to which they sub-vocalise words.

Why do we get stuck at those levels? Because that is the general expectation in society, and we assume that being able to read text and comprehend most of it is sufficient. In fact, most people are perfectly capable of tripling their reading speed to around 700–750 words per minute without a huge amount of effort.

Speed-reading is an expression that typically refers to reading significantly above 750 words per minute. However, the distinction between what is reading quickly and what is speed-reading is blurred and still subject to debate. Both the techniques and the results of speed-reading are very controversial. In particular, the trade-off between speed and comprehension rate has been discussed on many levels. The jury is still out on its benefits, but if you are interested, we would definitely recommend you to explore the field further.

Nevertheless, increasing your reading speed to at least 500 words per minute is the ultimate low hanging fruit, and you should definitely make sure that you pick it up. There are a number of books and software that help with improving one's reading speed; most of them focus on eliminating the three problems we have outlined previously and use the same or very similar techniques to achieve this.

We encourage you to type 'speed reading' into Amazon or Google and experiment; different things tend to work for different people. Nevertheless, if you are looking for a safe bet, try Tony Buzan's books. They provide a good overview and have received positive feedback across the world.

Secondly, how do you increase your typing speed? Touch-typing refers to typing with all ten fingers without using your sight to locate the keys. It is a relatively easy-to-learn skill which can improve your productivity dramatically. The average computer user types at approximately 33 words per minute, or roughly the same rate as fast handwriting.

Learning how to touch type will help you double that rate within a few weeks. Additional practice can then increase your speed even further – depending on how much time you spend typing every day and to what extent you focuses on consciously improving your speed in every day life, people frequently improve their speed to around 100 words per minute or even higher.

There are also some additional benefits that should not be overlooked – for one, being able to focus on thinking rather than locating the appropriate keys frees up brain time to increase your productivity even further.

Having said all of this, we need to warn you. Learning to touch type is one of the most tedious things you will do in your life – the process involves copious amounts of repetition in order to train your muscle memory which then allows you to subconsciously identify certain finger movements with letters, words and sentences. Nevertheless, the final payoff is definitely worth it.

Thirdly, how do you improve your memory? Memorising skills have taken a huge beating over the last few decades. Education systems in the West have shifted from memorising facts to learning how to interpret them. We became lazier as a society in memorising things – after all, what is the point if you can just always look it up on Google or Wikipedia?

The problem is that Google, dictionaries, encyclopaedias and other databases are only good for active search. What we mean by active search is that you know what you want to look up. If you know that you are interested in the capital of Ecuador, you can look it up and find out that it is Quito. But what if you want to decide where to base your new business?

Computers are generally only good with structured problems – you would need to define the criteria for what the best country for your business would look like, how important are they relative to each other, and most likely express the final problem as an equation. This does not sound like a good way of making business decisions, does it?

You could still make the decision yourself and just use a computer to look up the relevant information. This strategy has more merit, but you would still need to know what you are looking for. Unfortunately, many of the world's leading businessmen, academics or thinkers in general attribute their best decisions to a puzzle-like process where things just come together and start making sense, rather than as a result of some structured, easy-to-follow method.

The human mind is an extremely powerful tool capable of coming up with the most extraordinary theories and making great decisions. In order for the mind to be able to do that though, it needs certain inputs – facts and numbers – to be there already, present and latent, but ready to be recalled and analysed.

Think about it this way – if you have thousands and thousands of random facts stored in your brain, the mind can run through them and their combinations over and over and over at extremely fast pace, and use this processing capacity to reach the optimal decision or come up with an innovative idea. If, on the other hand, it needs to pause and ask you for more inputs every time it runs through such a loop, it will not be able to get through more than a fraction of the iterations.

This is how learning facts and numbers can make all the difference, and how our current education system falls short. The topic of memory improvement is far beyond the scope of this book, and again there are a number of resources available both offline and online.

Key Takeaways: Racing Against Time

- Time is the most precious resource you have as it can be exchanged readily for increases in your Four Accounts.

- Use the personal time matrix to evaluate the opportunity cost of your time, and reach a more productive distribution.

- Technology and computers take up a massive part of our daily productive time. Learn how to become more efficient with them early on so that you can focus on using these tools, rather than being enslaved by them.

- Reading, typing and memory retention are often overlooked as sources of outperformance. Do not follow the herd; invest into improving your skills in these areas in order to reap the benefits for the rest of your academic and professional career.

Don't forget the previous chapter: Mentors and Buddies

- Many successful people attribute their achievements to the help they have received from their mentors and buddies. These relationships provide an opportunity to learn from others and accelerate your own development.

- Find good buddies who will support you in your goals and vision. Focus on identifying people who are compatible – they should be on a similar level of achievement and motivation, and have complementary skills to your own.

- There are two approaches to finding mentors. Identify the areas where you want to work on yourself, and find people with the right experience and skills. Alternatively, find people who are just amazing, and go for it with the understanding that there is bound to be something they tan teach you.

- Converting potential mentors into real mentors can be quite difficult, especially if you aim very high. The best strategy is to show your passion, commitment and dedication, and try to spend more time with the person.

Chapter 15
Study Skills

"Live as if you would die tomorrow; learn as if you would live forever."

Mahatma Gandhi, political and spiritual leader

"Learning is not compulsory ... neither is survival."

W. Edwards Deming, statistician and innovator

Right, as this chapter is inevitably quite personal, I'm taking over entirely for the next few pages. Read on and you will see why.

Jan

15.1 Background

Working smart, rather than hard, will be the underlying theme of this chapter. For most goals, this strategy is more than sufficient. Working smart and hard will help you achieve the rest of the goals you might have. As I am about to give you some quite controversial advice, I guess it makes sense to begin by telling you a few anecdotes about my own experience with exams. Hopefully, they will help you understand where the advice that follows comes from.

The first story is about GCSEs. The Czech Republic ranks 5th in the world in science, 12th in Mathematics and 17th in reading skills of 15 year olds.[96] While I was at school there, I spent less than one hour per week learning, revising, doing my homework, or preparing for the various academic competitions I was involved in. Instead, I mostly entertained myself during classes by coming up with alternative proofs, methods and answers at best and mischief otherwise. In years ten and eleven, I took a laptop to most classes, and spent the time playing an online text-based strategic game I talked about earlier in the book.

I scored 13 A*s at the Czech GCSE-equivalent and received multiple awards in Mathematics, Physics and Informatics Olympiads.

The second story is about A-levels. I came to the UK in September 2004, barely speaking any English. In fact, when I went back to school to see my A-level Economics teacher during my first year at university, she admitted that things had been so bad when I had arrived that after our first lesson she had gone to see my tutor and told her that there was no way I could manage the material. My teacher strongly recommended that I switched to Chemistry or some other subject where my lack of language skills wouldn't be such a hindrance. My tutor fortunately convinced her otherwise.

18 months later and roughly ten weeks before my final exams, I decided to do ten A-levels rather than the seven I was doing at the time, as well as adding three Advanced Extension Awards (AEAs), formerly S-levels. Aside from having to learn the full syllabus in a few weeks, this meant that I sat 44 out of my 60 papers in the summer of 2006 rather than spreading them out across four sessions in two years as would normally be the case. It also meant that my exam timetable included several consecutive days with 10+ hours of exams each; I even had to be supervised overnight in certain instances.[97]

I still went on to get AAAAAAAAA at A-levels[98] and Distinctions in all 3 AEAs. More and above, I scored 100% in more than half of the papers I sat; my average was almost 96%[99], 16% higher than one needs for an A grade. My scores on the AEA papers were allegedly higher than any past papers my teachers had ever seen and well above the boundaries for Distinction grades.

The final story is about university. In my second year at university, I attended less than 5 out of the total 160 lectures for my courses. I was present in roughly 6 out of every 10 classes, and rarely handed in homework. Until April, I had no idea what-so-ever what we were meant to study – I did not buy textbooks, download the notes or pay any attention during the few classes I attended.

I started learning – learning, not revising – the material less than four weeks before my first exam, and worked on launching two businesses through the exam period, including coding, various meetings, copy writing and preparing the content. Nicube.com was launched two days after my last exam. My revision tactic was to take the courses one after the other, in the order in which my exams were scheduled. This would leave me around three to five days between every two papers.

My last two exams were Linear Algebra and Calculus, scheduled for Monday afternoon and Thursday morning, respectively. I finished an exam on Thursday the week before, and then spent Friday, Saturday and Sunday learning and revising for the Linear Algebra paper. On Monday morning, at about 10:30am, 4 hours before the Linear Algebra paper, I decided to check the venue, and looked at my timetable. My heart rate exploded, and for several seconds I thought "This cannot be true. This sort of stuff only happens in movies."

It was true. The exam scheduled for 2.30pm that afternoon was Calculus, a course I had not even seen – let alone learnt, revised or practised – since November of the previous year. I panicked for a minute, and then thought "Screw it – let's see what can be done".

I printed out the course notes, a few past papers and solutions. I went through the 302 pages of notes and threw every page that was not absolutely critical for the exam into the bin. In my first reading, I reduced the course to 35 pages. I went through the notes again, and got them down to 16.

I then read those notes carefully. I looked at past paper questions, briefly tried to run through my thoughts about how to solve them in my head, and then checked the official solutions. I finished at about 1pm. I decided that more learning was not going to do me any good, and that having a proper lunch before the exam would be a better idea. I grabbed some food, and then left home for the LSE to sit my exam, finishing off three days later with the Linear Algebra paper.

I still scored a First class.

Right now (April 2009), 6 weeks before my finals, exams still have priority of seven or thereabouts on my list. I am working at a hedge fund and writing this book, preparing to get it edited, type set, designed, printed, distributed and marketed.

I am managing my companies – in June, we are launching Sucedo, a new start-up that will level the playing field for university applicants who come from schools which do not provide the same level of advice and support as others.

I am also launching a new marketing campaign and adding a range of new services on Nicube.com, planning our expansion outside of Oxford and Cambridge at CrewDates, and AlphaParties has just had the best start of the year ever. Halfway through my exams I will be sitting professional exams in finance & economics ahead of starting work full-time.

Is this riskier than focusing exclusively on exams? Absolutely. Is it also more rewarding? Undoubtedly.

15.2 How to learn effectively

Let's make a very clear distinction right from the start – there is a big difference between learning effectively and revising/ sitting exams effectively. While these are obviously not mutually exclusive, neither of them implies the other.

In other words, being able to learn effectively does not mean that you can revise and perform well in exams. Conversely, as much as our schools and universities would like to have you believe otherwise, being able to do well in exams does not mean that you have learnt and understood the material. Arguably exams are a half-decent proxy for judging how well you have grasped the material, but this proxy is by no means perfect. For one, exams by their design favour people with good memories over those with other skills – their results are therefore biased in this way.

I therefore split the study skills material into two chapters – this one talks about how to learn effectively. The following chapter then looks at techniques, methods and strategies that can help you revise effectively and perform well in exams.

Effective learning can be boiled down to a few basic factors – a) understanding your objectives, i.e. what you want to get out of it b) creating the right high-level plan, i.e. strategy c) executing well, i.e. tactics.

These three aspects determine your performance when it comes to learning. I am not ruling out that there are more detailed strategies and further tips and methods – what I am are doing is focusing on the 20% of habits that can help you achieve the 80% of the available results, or in other words finding the most efficient and leveraged way of improving your performance in learning.

1. Understand your objectives

Most of you will remember situations when you spent two hours reading a textbook and when you got to the end of the chapter, you did not really know what it contained and whether you learnt anything at all. This happens to many students all the time. Reading a book over and over again with no specific goal or purpose is one of the least efficient ways of learning.

Your brain likes anchors – specific points or key data and information that can be used to create the basic framework of understanding. So it is important to define objectives before you start learning so that your brain has key points around which it can group other information and a way of evaluating its performance.

How do you define objectives? Imagine you are reading a book for your literature classes. What do you want to remember or know when you finish? Do you want to have a view on the sentence structure of the book? The narrative method? A detailed understanding of the characters, their backgrounds, interactions and motives? Or something else altogether? It is only when you know what you are trying to get out of reading the book that you can start focusing on these aspects, both consciously and subconsciously.

Equivalently, if you are studying from your chemistry notes, there are several different areas you might want to focus on. Do you want to have a very good understanding of how the high level concepts interlink? Do you need to memorize specific examples, formulas, or equations? Do you need to be able to prove certain things, or derive them from scratch?

Defining your objectives helps you focus and keep your concentration levels high during your studies. In addition, it creates immediate benchmarks and feedback loops. If you do not have objectives, how do you determine if you need to re-read a particular chapter? The only criterion you have in such a situation is whether you feel that you understand the material or not. That is a pretty unreliable benchmark.

2. Always have a high-level strategic plan

Being able to execute well is of very little use unless you know where you are going, and the other way round. There are many students who perform well in implementation or in strategic planning. There are very few who can do both well, but it is only when you combine these two factors that you see the really steep increase in your performance.

Strategic planning is about mapping out the journey ahead and setting clear expectations in order to ensure a smooth, effective execution later on. To be more specific – once you have decided on your objectives, you need to use these to create the right strategy for learning the material.

If you want to learn how to speak a new language to a certain level, set a deadline – even if it is two years ahead. Next, divide the time between now and then into logical periods, perhaps corresponding to your terms or structure of your classes. Then set intermediate objectives so that at any point in time, you know what should be your focus at that time. Get your teacher involved in this planning process if you need expert help.

The key distinction between hardworking students and smart-working students is actually not practice but what Malcolm Gladwell calls 'deliberate practice'.[100] Deliberate practice is about identifying the areas where you want to improve, and then consciously working on them at the edge of your ability.

Where the hardworking student will download all study notes, homework exercise sets and past papers and diligently work through all of them from start to end, the smart student will download the latest past paper, work through it, and then re-evaluate. She will identify areas that need improving, and then work on those specifically, pushing herself further every time. Although she will, *ceteris paribus*, probably spend less than 50% of time revising and learning than the hardworking student, she is likely to do at least as well, and most likely better, when it comes to exams.

The difference between the two students is that the hardworking student works and thinks hard about the content but is mentally lazy when it comes to thinking about how to approach the studying process itself. Working your way through an exercise set one problem after another is in many ways more comforting/easier than pushing yourself consciously on some of them. It just requires you to start working and keep doing so until you finish.

The smart working student is the opposite – perhaps a bit lazy or at least not overly proactive when it comes to volume of what she studies. She is, however, extremely hardworking when it comes to thinking about how to work, planning the schedule, evaluating her performance, and correcting it during the process.

Always consider the big picture first. Decide on deadlines and benchmarks. Divide the work into smaller pieces – this has the added benefit of making it feel like you are learning effortlessly. If you, for example, set aside just 15–30min every day as opposed to two hours thrice a week, learning will eventually feel much easier and much less like hard work. Develop a deliberate practice plan, rather than a hardworking one. Continue evaluating whether you are learning effectively, and adjust the course if necessary.

3. Use the right tactics

While strategy concerns itself with the 60,000 feet view of things, tactics is really about the small, day-to-day things that determine how you execute your plan. Most of you will have had extensive experience with various methods, some of which worked well and others perhaps not so well. What follows is a summary of what I believe to be some of the most powerful techniques around, particularly with respect to the relative effort required and reward/outcome produced:

a) Remove distractions and create an environment conductive to learning

It's obvious stuff but actually do it: switch off your computers. Facebook Chat/MSN and learning do not really go well together. Put the phone on silent. Switch off the TV. If you have to work on a computer, switch off every distracting application, and try to sustain the self-control and discipline to avoid web browsing, game playing etc.

Only leave music on provided you are 100% sure it does not distract you. Close your door. Ask your friends not to disturb you for an hour unless the matter is urgent. Make sure you are not hungry or thirsty and will not use that as an excuse to slack off when you get bored. Get a bottle of water. And so on. I know the advice itself is very simple – but following it can actually be quite hard.

b) Focus on understanding and do not compromise

If you do not understand something, immediately clarify – ask your teacher, research the topic, do anything it takes. A great way of clarifying concepts or ideas is often checking their definitions with several teachers, friends or books. Small gaps in understanding can grow into massive black holes and cause much more stress later on.

This is an area where most people make mistakes, regardless of whether they are studying history, languages, physics or pure mathematics. It is particularly important in sciences, however, never to compromise on your understanding – you must always seek to understand the full proof or concept without relying on getting back to it later. Thinking "I will look it up later" never works. Learning is a cumulative process – you need to build the basics first before proceeding higher.

c)   Develop intuition, particularly in technical subjects

In mathematics, what is a derivative? If you try answering with an equation, you probably did not quite understand the concept. You have to be able to visualise the entire idea in plain language, with examples that a child could understand. The same applies for virtually every other concept, not only in mathematics but across all fields. One of the few things shared by the best and brightest minds of history is that they all developed and thought about concepts in an extremely intuitive way.[101] You cannot combine different mathematical concepts in order to prove something if you only understand the individual parts separately, as equations rather than intuitive concepts.

The same applies to other subjects – you must develop intuition, the skill of being able to understand without abstract reasoning. This makes things more natural and allows you to step up and start thinking about the more difficult things. If you can get the basics working naturally, you have 100% of your brain power to focus on the real challenges. If, on the other hand, you always need to go back to definitions and look things up/write them down in order to understand them, you will repeatedly waste time and energy that could be used more productively elsewhere.

To illustrate this with an example, consider multiplication. Intuition is all about taking a concept that is difficult to grasp, and interpreting it using what we already know. Do you still remember how you were taught multiplication at school? Most likely, the teacher explained it in terms of addition – something you already knew because you had learnt it before. Multiplication can be thought of as a shortcut for repeated addition. You would be surprised how easy many concepts in advanced mathematics and many other fields become when you think about them in this way.

d) Understand how memory works, and make use of it

We know today that when we first hear about something, our memory decays at an exponential rate. On an intuitive level, if you encounter a new concept for the first time and there are 100 or more things to remember about it, you may start forgetting them at a rate of 10% of what you remember per week. Initially, you remember 100. After one week, this goes down by 10% of 100, i.e. 10, so you remember 90. After another week, this goes down by 10% of 90, i.e. 9, so you remember 81, and so on. The percentage itself varies – it depends on your memorisation skills and how interesting or important the subject seemed to your brain.

But when you hear, read, or talk about something for the second time, this not only brings your memory retention back to its previous level, it also changes the rate of decay. What happens when you read about the concept again when you are at 90 is that you bring up your understanding back to perhaps 98, but more importantly, your rate of forgetting drops, say to 5%. This means that you are now forgetting things at a dramatically slower rate. Just to illustrate – if you are forgetting at a 10% rate, you will remember less than 35% of the original after only 10 weeks. If the rate of forgetting slows down to 5%, however, you will still remember almost 60% after 10 weeks.

What is the practical application? When you read or generally learn something new, you should revisit the concept the day after, then one week after, then two weeks after and then a month after. This will dramatically increase the amount of information you will retain in your memory, and even more importantly, it will significantly reduce the rate at which you are now forgetting this information.

Obviously, this all ties very well with the strategic planning as the person who is aware of all these things (the need to develop intuition, make use of memory cycles etc.) will plan his strategy in a way that facilitates these tactics. For example, if you start learning one week before exams, it is almost impossible to develop intuition unless you are very good at a given subject. If you start, however, spending 15 minutes on the subject every other day 10 months before your exam, you will have plenty of time to think things through, ask good questions and develop a real understanding.

If you start learning one week before the exam, you cannot make use of the power of repeated study and its impact on memory retention. Having the discipline to plan properly and follow up on the plan can make your life significantly easier and save you many hours that you will otherwise spend cramming on the night before the exam. In addition, it is much more difficult to add concepts learnt over a very short period of time to your long-term memory.

e) It's not rocket science

What I tell you is actually very simple, but that is the point about effective learning – it is both difficult and easy. The methods are often easy; the implementation and adoption of new habits and techniques is not. The point of this chapter, really, is to present the ideas in a condensed manner that will make it difficult for you to find an excuse not to do them. Do not read this, think "Yes, that makes sense" and then go on falling asleep over your textbook!

15.3   How to perform well in exams

Designing an exam that perfectly tests your understanding is impossible, or very difficult at best. The good news is that as a consequence, exams tend to be pretty standardised and repeat the same format every year and actually also across different schools, curriculums and universities. There are a number of things we know about how they are written, answered and marked. It really makes sense to take advantage of them.

The following statement is very important to understanding how to do well in exams – getting As is not about demonstrating your grasp of the subject. Getting As is about producing work that meets whatever benchmarks and standards have been set by the examining institution.

Real understanding is not something that has clearly defined rules and boundaries – in fact, leading academics of today, as well as throughout history in general, have often become famous for stepping outside of what was accepted in their field at the time. Academia and research are actually the opposite of high school or undergraduate teaching in many ways. The former rewards innovation and stepping outside the box. The latter rewards conforming to clearly defined rules and delivering on what is required.

The first piece of advice is simple – understand the game, and learn as much as possible about its rules. You would not try to compete in rugby without finding out the rules of the game first. You would not try to fly a plane without getting qualified. Yet most students feel quite comfortable playing the exam game without understanding its rules properly.

Who writes the papers? Is it the lecturer, someone from the university/school, or someone else altogether? Can you find out who it is? If so, can you get hold of their previous work, be it papers or books? Can you find out more about their views on teaching? Can you get hold of past exam papers and past exam solutions? Can you get hold of past examiners reports, or summaries of students' performance? Can you obtain copies of marked scripts of other people? Can you get a feeling for the feedback given to last year's cohort after they sat the exams and got results?

These are all highly relevant questions. When I started learning for the three A-levels and three extension papers I decided to pick up only a few weeks before my exams, the first thing I did before even looking at the textbook was to get hold of examiner's reports for these subjects and read through them.

Know your enemy. Read as much as you can about the exam itself, its structure and its grading, who wrote it and who is marking it. Find out what made people stand out, and what sunk their chances in the past.

Trust me, most teachers and academics have more interesting things to do than designing exams. As far as structure and marking is concerned, exams are repetitive. The same, in fact, often applies to content, even if it is dressed up slightly differently. Take advantage of this repetition. Research everything properly. It can take a few hours but the payoff is well worth it. Once you understand what you need to do and what not to do, the game becomes a lot easier.

Second, do not try to write a world-changing essay or revolutionise quantum physics in your exam. Most exams are standardized. They all get marked to the same marking scheme; innovation and originality rarely get any points. Sad but true; do not waste your effort and chances. Produce the consistent, predictable, high quality answers that your examiners are looking for.

There are many better opportunities for your innovative work. Unless you are extremely confident about your abilities in a given subject, have high tolerance for risk and are willing to gamble on getting 'enlightened' examiners, exams should be about writing down what you already know and have done well before.

Giving 'unusual' answers exposes you to high risk without giving you much extra rewards compared to giving expected, but high-quality answers that the examiners are looking for. Adjust your strategy accordingly.

Third, manage energy and attention, not just time. Most people see time as the ultimate scarce resource and they are partially right. We may have all the time in the world, but our ability to focus is definitely limited. Bear this in mind when you devise your revision strategy, as well as strategy for tackling the exam itself.

Fourth, realise that you have plenty of time and do not panic. Time pressure should not be a problem in most exams, provided that you tackle them well. This is especially true for A-levels and similar qualifications. The biggest mistake you can make is thinking that you must spend 100% of your time producing output and writing stuff down – in fact, this is a very good way to underperforming relative to your potential.

What happens is that either you misread the question and do not answer it properly or you go off tangentially because you are frantically writing rather than thinking about how to structure your arguments and pick up the points. Alternatively, especially in science subjects, you will make a basic (possibly arithmetical) mistake that will invalidate your entire argument and require ten minutes to discover and fix.

Do a mock exam. Realise how much time you have. Use it wisely, plan ahead, write a plan for the essay or the proof that you are asked about, and then execute well.

The act of writing down the answer should not be one of creation. If you are writing an essay, your facts, definition, arguments, theories, and quotes should already be on the page, and you should be only compiling and combing them.

If you are proving a mathematical theorem, the individual steps should already be clearly decided and planned, and you should only be connecting those dots.

Fifth, focus on what scores points and do not waste time on what does not. It is imperative that your handwriting is legible; as all examiners across qualifications and degrees confirm, illegible handwriting has probably lost students more marks than any other mistake.

If your exams involve a lot of writing, get a good fountain pen – it naturally makes your handwriting more legible and your wrist more relaxed, avoiding any cramps. Having written 40 pages in three hours for my S-level papers, I am speaking from experience here.

On the other hand, as long as your writing is legible, it does not matter if you cross every other line. Do not obsess about cosmetic details – the examiners want to read your paper, but they understand the time constraints of an exam. As long as your diagrams are clear, they do not need to be in five different colours. Throw away your ruler.

A common myth is that the quality of your writing matters on these exams. This is rarely true. Unless you are writing an exam in a language or other subject where quality of writing matters, do not waste too much time on style. Beautifully crafted sentences do not get points – substance, facts, content and arguments do.

Sixth, prepare for the predictable. There are very few educational institutions in the world that like having students fail exams. This means that the first 40–50% of marks on most exams are available to a trained monkey with some memory. Do not be the student who scores the other 50% and leaves the easy marks on the table. Learn your definitions. Learn the predictable arguments, and remember the facts, quotes and theories that come up year after year.

Seventh, most 200 page courses can be reduced into fewer than ten pages. Read your course notes one to three times, depending on your memory and speed of thinking. Then read them again, but every time you come across a page that is 'non-core' to the course, rip it off and bin it.

Go through the entire pack of notes in this way. Then do it again. And again. Eventually, you should end up with a small pack of highly relevant notes that effectively summarize the content of the course. Learning these well and nothing else is probably good enough for an A/high B already. Spice things up with some extra reading and you should comfortably score the highest grades.

Eighth, do not listen to that voice in your head saying "well this might be useful ... well, I better learn this just in case". The reason why so many students underperform in exams is because they do not have the intellectual independence to say "I do not need to know this". Most people obsess about understanding and remembering every detail of the course, regardless of its relevance or importance.

Your resources (time and attention) are limited. Understanding core principles well is better than knowing everything shallowly. Most exams are predictable, regardless of whether they are in sciences or arts. Many exams involve choice. If this is the case, learning the key principles well will usually allow you to pick questions you like and answer them very well.

Aim to develop an intuition about what you do and do not need to learn. Be selective. Do not waste time learning what you can deduce. Devoting time to practising remote concepts when you do not understand the core will not prepare you well. Discerning the essential from the interesting is difficult, especially when you are under pressure. Be brutal – begin to trust your intuition of what is important and it will become easier with practice.

There is no way that you will have the time and opportunity to write everything you know about the subject in an exam. So do not waste time and effort on learning every single marginal detail unless is directly relevant to one of the core themes.

Key Takeaways: Study Skills

- Study smart rather than hard. That way, you give yourself space to push harder when you really need to.

- There is a big difference between learning effectively and revising/sitting exams effectively. While these are obviously not mutually exclusive, neither implies the other. Understand if your purpose is learning or sitting exams, and adopt the right strategy.

- Effective learning comes down to three key things: understand your objectives, create the right high-level plan (strategy) and execute well (tactics).

- Doing well in exams is not about demonstrating your grasp of the subject but rather about producing work that meets given benchmarks and standards, set by the examining institution. Accept that exams are a game, understand it and learn as much as possible about its rules.

Don't forget the previous chapter: Racing Against Time

- Time is the most precious resource you have as it can be exchanged readily for increases in your Four Accounts.

- Use the personal time matrix to evaluate the opportunity cost of your time, and reach a more productive distribution.

- Technology and computers take up a massive part of our daily productive time. Learn how to become more efficient with them early on so that you can focus on using these tools, rather than being enslaved by them.

- Reading, typing and memory retention are often overlooked as sources of outperformance. Do not follow the herd; invest into improving your skills in these areas in order to reap the benefits for the rest of your academic and professional career.

Chapter 16
Thinking Outside the Box

"The difficulty lies not in the new ideas, but in escaping from the old ones, which ramify, for those brought up as most of us have been, into every corner of our minds."

John Maynard Keynes, economist

"There are no statues erected to critics."

Timothy Ferris, author and productivity expert

16.1   What does thinking outside the box mean?

Thinking outside the box, often also described to as lateral thinking, refers to thinking unconventionally, differently or from an entirely new perspective. To explain the origin of the expression, let's look at a puzzle. The following diagram involves nine dots arranged in a 3 × 3 square grid. The challenge is to connect the dots by drawing four straight, continuous lines without ever lifting the pen from the paper.

Try the challenge, and give it some thought. If you can solve it, well done – you are likely to either have seen it before, or be a natural lateral thinker. If you cannot, do not worry – most people fit into this category. The solution is presented on the next page.

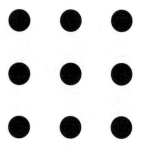

The reason most people fail even though the solution is very easy is that the solution is only easy when you consider possibilities that involve drawing outside of the area defined by the square of the nine dots. Because of the way we are used to thinking, most people never venture outside of the box when looking for solutions. This puzzle allegedly gave the name to the idea of thinking differently, after it became popular in the consultancy circles.[102]

As business and academia have become more competitive, being able to ignore or bypass traditional restrictions and barriers, and come up with answers and solutions that are not immediately obvious and arise from non-obvious thought patterns has come to be considered one of the most important skills in many professions – and not just those that would normally be seen as creative.

16.2   How to think outside the box

How do you describe and structure something that is by definition difficult to replicate? Fortunately, there are a number of things we can do and techniques we can adopt in order to increase the chances of stumbling upon a good idea. Certain people, companies, groups and other organisations have proved over the years that unconventional ideas do not occur entirely at random, and that we can influence this process. Although it is different for every individual, experimentation is key; here are some experiments to get you going.

1. Read a lot

Read lots and from a variety of genres. Reading books is like cheating – you are getting advice and life experience from some of the greatest minds of humanity. If you read great books, you can learn quicker and more effectively and avoid making mistakes that others have already made.

2. Question everything

Most advancements in our civilisation happened when someone looked at something that was considered a given at the time and challenged whether it really had to be the case. This applies to sciences as well as to industry.

3. Learn how to fail well and often

Thinking differently means being different and exploring ideas and concepts that have not been tried before. Inevitably, this process involves failing more often than others. Thomas Edison once said *"I have not failed. I've just found 10,000 ways that won't work."* when talking about his invention of a light bulb.

It is natural that we do not like making mistakes. We have always been told off for making them at school, university and work, and taught to avoid them. Unfortunately for innovation, feeling bad about mistakes is a hard-coded behavioural pattern for most people by the time they leave high school. But mistakes make it possible to learn, grow and develop, and so should be valued, provided that we got to them in a productive way. Accept failure as a part of the process and way of getting feedback, and learn how to celebrate your failures.

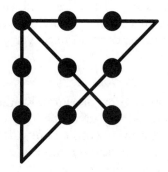

4. Expose yourself to randomness. Do crazy things

We gave the background to this principle earlier when talking about networking and the idea here is very similar. You cannot think differently if you do what everyone else does.

Take crazy class combinations. Are you a mathematician? Take classes on sociology of apes in the rainforest. Are you majoring in English or History? Dabble in discrete mathematics. Go to conferences on the weirdest topics. Read random blogs. Go to Wikipedia and click on 'random article' until you find something interesting that opens your mind.

5. Write down all your ideas

We talked earlier about the way our mind can sometimes work, shooting down ideas before seriously considering them. Do not let this mechanism hold you back. Whenever you think of something interesting, whether revolutionary or quite banal, write it down. Paper is cheap and you can always use your mobile or computer. Write down all your ideas, and go through them once every week to figure out if any of them are worth pursuing. Coming back to your ideas days after you had them rather than deciding on their validity right away will allow you to consider their merits and potential more rationally.

6. Build curiosity

Learn how to become naturally inquisitive about everyday things as well as harder academic or business concepts. Learn to think about how things work, and why they work.

One of the best ways of building curiosity is to assume that everything is interesting for a month, even those things that would normally be considered boring by everyone. Try it for a month and see what comes out. Curiosity allows you to go that extra mile and dig deeper than other people, because it makes you naturally eager to learn, and enjoy the process of learning.

7. Do the important, not the urgent

Constantly focusing on whatever is urgent at the time while leaving the important, non-urgent things slip into the urgent, important box is a great way to never have time to give anything your very best. Many people never excel in anything because they do not give themselves the time to produce their very best.

Give yourself full two weeks to write that essay. Think it through, explore and read around the topic. If you always start writing and researching the night before, you will never produce your best work, and perhaps never discover the passion you could have otherwise developed for the subject.

8. Start thinking about the stuff you read

Question it, analyse it and make connections with what you already know. Most of us read passively – we just go through the text and mechanically read it. Becoming engaged with whatever you are reading, and actively questioning its accuracy, relating it to other concepts you already know from the same as well as different areas and asking the right questions will massively increase the benefit you get from reading anything, whether newspapers, textbooks or books.

9. Have lots of ideas

As it turns out, having lots of ideas is one of the best predictors of having good ideas. *"The strongest correlation for quality of ideas is, in fact, quantity of ideas … Pablo Picasso, for instance, produced 20,000 pieces of art; Einstein wrote more than 240 papers; Bach wrote a cantata every week; Thomas Edison filed a record 1,039 patents."*[103]

10. Know your intellectual environment

We stand on the shoulders of those who came before us. If you do not follow leading experts in your field, you cannot expect to come up with any revolutionary innovations. If you are standing on the shoulders of giants of 1950s while everyone else is standing on those of contemporary leaders, you will not be able to compete.

11. Seek the same diversity in people as you seek in ideas

Do not underestimate the impact of our cultural, ethnic, educational, and professional background on the way we identify opportunities, look at situations, analyse problems and come up with answers. Make sure that your teams and organisations involve a wide range of people from different backgrounds so that someone can bridge a gap in thinking when everyone else fails.

In one way, this is a way of achieving the same outcomes as having diverse interests, but in a much more leveraged way. But there is more to it. Assume that person A is heterosexual, Chinese, male and Buddhist. Person B is gay, white British, female and atheist. Even if A could learn everything that B knows, he still would not be able to add the same value to the team – and vice versa. It is not only diversity of knowledge and interests that has benefits – the same applies to diversity of backgrounds.

12. Do not be afraid of solitude, and seek it on a regular basis

Some of the most successful innovators and scientists in history have attributed much of their success to the time spent in quiet reflection. Being able to separate yourself from other people allows you to stop listening and passively receiving their thoughts, and start exploring your own.

13. Be intellectually independent

This means separating out your sense of self-worth from the opinion of others on your ideas and beliefs. The only way to become a truly independent thinker is to convince your brain that while opinions of others should be valued and taken into account, they say nothing about the worth of yourself as a person.

14. Get a well rounded education

If you have or are specialising at school and then university, make up for the deficiencies in other areas by exploring them independently. Ensure that you have a basic level of understanding in all major fields of human activity – history, languages, geography, economics, mathematics, physics, chemistry, music, arts, sociology, psychology, anatomy etc.

This relates back to what we said earlier about memory – having a broad overview and understanding of different disciplines, rather than just the ability to find out about them when needed, will allow you to actually think and make decisions that involve multiple areas. You will be able to draw connections between these different disciplines and leverage them in your decision making process. Having diverse interests allows you to look at things from a fresh perspective.

15. Do one thing every day that irrationally scares you/is new

Following this advice is the best way of ensuring that you do something you would not have done otherwise. This re-creates old neural pathways, or even better creating completely new ones, and can help you start thinking in completely new dimensions. Many physicists and mathematicians enjoy playing a musical instrument because this very different type of activity helps to open up and start using an entirely different and new part of their brain.[104]

Fortunately, stimulating those parts of your brain that are normally active when you are being creative is relatively simple – they get activated when you experience something new.[105]

16.3 How to use thinking outside the box to make better decisions in life

Many of the world's leading entrepreneurs, academics, leaders, inventors and scientists have repeatedly confirmed that coming up with the right questions is a key skill in both the innovation process and good decision making. Knowing the right questions is the first step to knowing the right answers.

What follows are questions and mind games that we have found particularly provocative when it comes to making decisions about one's life. These are the sort of questions you may want to ask yourself when making difficult life choices, but also every now and then just to make sure you are on the right track. They play the devil's advocate.

Interesting questions

1. Imagine that you won a lottery and the money was enough to support you and your family on a very comfortable lifestyle for the rest of your life, with one condition – you must never take up paid employment again. How would you spend the rest of your life?

2. Imagine you were always on camera. We are not talking about being on a reality TV show, but imagine that there would be a permanent public record of everything you do or say from now on that anyone in the world could view at anytime. How would you change your behaviour?[106]

3. What would you do if you were told that you were terminally ill and could only expect to live for another six months? How would you spend those months? Why cannot you spend the following six months like that regardless?

4. Where do you live? Where would you like to live? Are the two places different? If so, why? Give real reasons, no excuses.

5. Imagine you were to receive a hundred times your current/expected salary for the rest of your life with one condition – this would be taken away forever if you felt unhappy for a single day. What would you do with the rest of your life?

6. Imagine you got into the best university in the world, but then the university changed its rules and said that when you graduate, you must never disclose your results and

nobody would ever know about them. You could only say if you passed or failed. How would you spend your time at university compared to how you spend it otherwise?

7. What if, regardless of what work you do, your salary was directly determined by how happy you feel while in the office? How would that change your career choices?

8. What if all your best friends suddenly forgot you ever existed and you had to rebuild your friends circles from scratch. Would you still become best friends with the same people? If not, why don't you change your friends now?

9. Imagine you could decide to do anything you want for the next two years and some divine power would guarantee that you cannot fail in it. What would you do?

10. Imagine you were told that you must never work again for anyone else in your life. What sort of business would you start?

11. Imagine your parents forgot what subjects you were doing at school or what degree you read at university, you could never tell them and they could never find out again. Would that change your choices? If so, why?

12. What would you do for the next ten years if you knew that the world is going to reset and go back to the state it is in today in ten years?

13. Pick your biggest weakness. Imagine you did not have it. How would that change your life? If significantly, can you reduce that weakness or get rid of it completely?

14. Imagine you entered a competition for $100 million. The winner would be the person who becomes the best in the world in any discipline. What would you do?

15. What was the last positive thing that would not let you fall asleep, and would make you jump out of bed in the morning and not feel tired? Is it a big part of your life today? If not, why not?

16. What would your friends and family put in your epitaph? Do you like it? If not, what are you going to do about it?

17. When was the last time you felt pure happiness? What were you doing at the time? How often do you do this?

18. Imagine you would be forced to wear a device that prevents you not only from lying, but also from saying half-truths and not saying something you know the other party wouldn't like to hear. Would this change your life significantly? If so, is there something you should change?

19. Imagine that employers around the world would be legally prohibited from ever asking about your track record, university and employment history, achievements etc. The only selection tool for recruiting would be motivational letters and interviews. How would that change your chances and your behaviour? Would your chances improve or are you just a walking CV?

The list goes on – you can come up with your own questions, or play a similar game with your friends, mentors or buddies. What we have hopefully achieved is to help you understand that well-structured questions can lead to unexpected conclusions that are difficult to reach otherwise.

Well structured and thought-through questions make us look at things from a different point of view, drop certain assumptions or falsely held beliefs, and help us crystallize our views and consider the real costs of our actions. This is why they are so important, and why you should always seek to actively make use of them and come up with those that are relevant to your own life when making hard decisions.

Key Takeaways: Thinking Outside the Box

- Thinking outside the box means thinking unconventionally, differently or from an entirely new perspective. It is the ability to ignore or bypass traditional restrictions and barriers, and come up with answers and solutions that are not immediately obvious and arise from non-obvious thought patterns.

- It is difficult to describe and structure something that is by definition hard to replicate. Nevertheless, there are a number of things you can do and techniques you can adopt in order to increase the chances of stumbling upon a good idea.

- Learn how to come up with good questions. This is a key skill for innovation and effective decision making. Knowing the right questions is the first step to knowing the right answers.

- Thinking outside the box can provide some questions that directly help to improve your own decision making about your life – make use of them.

Don't forget the previous chapter: Study Skills

- Study smart rather than hard. That way, you give yourself space to push harder when you really need to.

- There is a big difference between learning effectively and revising/sitting exams effectively. While these are obviously not mutually exclusive, neither implies the other. Understand if your purpose is learning or sitting exams, and adopt the right strategy.

- Effective learning comes down to three key things: understand your objectives, create the right high-level plan (strategy) and execute well (tactics).

- Doing well in exams is not about demonstrating your grasp of the subject but rather about producing work that meets given benchmarks and standards, set by the examining institution. Accept that exams are a game, understand it and learn as much as possible about its rules.

Chapter 17
Productive Leisure

"The best intelligence test is what we do with our leisure."

Laurence J. Peter, educator

"The reading of all good books is like conversation with the finest men of past centuries."

René Descartes, philosopher and mathematician

17.1 The peculiarity of human leisure

It is one of the ubiquities of the human race, and certainly the most remarkable one to us, spanning religions, geographies, ethnicities and social-economic groups, that leisure can be broadly described as doing things that are not beneficial for us, or that do not increase our four accounts. With some notable exceptions, people in the West, and to a large extent in other cultures too, spend their leisure time doing things that are at best neutral, and at worst outright detrimental.

The following two people are real. We have changed the names, and condensed everything into a single weekend to highlight the differences, but that is it. These stories are true reflections of lifestyles lead by two men who are otherwise very similar, coming from very similar backgrounds and studying at the same university. It hopefully highlights that

a) relatively small lifestyle changes can lead to enormously different outcomes, and

b) it is entirely possible to enjoy a full social life whilst accomplishing more.

4pm, Friday. James finishes his last class, and rings up his mates to find out what they are up to. Inevitably, most of them will be hanging around in one of the pubs on or around campus. He goes to an event on campus first where the guest speaker is the United States Ambassador, but he finds it quite hard to get much from the meeting. He stays despite this, out of some sense of it being the right way to spend his time. He then catches his mates for a few pints and smokes a few cigarettes standing outside the overcrowded venue. He and his friends talk about the same things over and over again.

Around 7–8pm, they get hungry. None of them have booked a decent place to go so they end up, as usual, at one of their favourite joints – a kebab shop full of greasy, undercooked meat. They have a bite, and start wondering about what to do next – James' friends start calling others to see what they are doing tonight. The odds are it will take them an hour or two to finish arguing about where to go.

They finally head to a club where most of their other friends already got in. By the time they get there, a massive queue has formed outside the venue, or alternatively their friends have moved somewhere else. When they finally get in it is around 11.30pm. The music is too loud to have a decent conversation. They wait around for an hour, have some more drinks, dance a bit, and eventually decide to do something else. They leave the venue, and start discussing other options – invariably they disagree and different people's varying alcohol levels mean that the group might break into smaller groups. His mate Paul has had too much to drink, is vomiting and needs to be carried home. James and some others head to the nearest fast food joint to have even more greasy unhealthy grub, hang around, and then head home. Having made a fool of himself several times during the evening by trying to pull that pretty friend of his classmates', James fails again to take her home.

The next day James had signed up to attend a conference organised by an international think-tank, as he found some topics on the agenda of interest and thought it may help him think about plans after university. The conference is free to students as it is sponsored by two multinational companies. However, he wakes up at 2pm with a horrible hangover, feeling sick from the junk food he ate last night, and, having missed half the conference, remains bed-ridden. He switches on the TV, and orders in food for a late lunch. He watches the TV until 4pm when he intends to do some work, but his friends call him at 5, and they go on to repeat yesterday's experience. Sunday is mostly spent recovering from the excesses of the previous two nights, watching TV and wasting hours discussing the trivial events of the last two days on Facebook and MSN.

Two years later, James leaves university having fortunately

scraped a low Upper Second class degree, but with a near-empty CV and little idea of what to do next.

4pm, Friday. Nick finishes his last class and attends a talk at his university's International Relations Society by an ambassador from the American Embassy who is visiting the university. He then grabs a quick coffee with the ambassador as it was actually Nick who invited him along being the society's Events Officer. They have an interesting conversation about anything and everything, quickly moving off politics onto extreme sports and skiing resorts, and agree to have a lunch at some future date.

Nick mentions a couple of books that he recently read on American politics when working on his dissertation thesis, and that he is planning to visit the States in the summer. The ambassador mentions that they actually recently opened a new internship programme for several think-tanks in Washington, DC, and offers to recommend Nick's application. Six months later, Nick ends up taking part in the programme, having the time of his life enjoying a summer in Washington DC, the highlight being attending a seminar where Barack Obama speaks.

Around 6pm, Nick heads home, quickly checks afternoon news and responds to urgent e-mails before getting ready to leave half an hour later. He joins a group of his friends at the Latino Dance Society, and after two hours of having fun trying some new salsa and meringue moves, they move on to a new Peruvian restaurant that one of his friends had recently discovered. They planned the evening, so actually have a booking in place. Several other friends join them for the dinner. The group is fairly diverse in its views on everything from football and food to current affairs and music, so the conversation is often heated, but never boring. They continue the dialogue at a nearby jazz bar without getting plastered into the early hours.

On Saturday morning, Nick wakes up at 10am to head out to the conference that James missed. Expected topics for debate include climate change, the rise of China and India in today's economy, and the importance of family in today's society. Some of the world's leading experts on these topics are taking part in a panel discussion as well as a lively debate with the audience. He meets a number of new and interesting people at the conference, and bumps into several old friends. They seem to be pretty organised, preparing their applications for internships this summer whether in politics, media, finance or philanthropy.

Nick needs to leave early to attend a dinner organised by his girlfriend, and rings her to check if he can bring two extra guests along from the conference, and shortly all three of them head over to the restaurant. His girlfriend is a foodie extraordinaire, and has used her knowledge of the scene and contacts to negotiate a special deal at a great discount with an up-and-coming restaurant. A month later the manager asks her to be his restaurant's promoter for the student crowd offering quite a generous salary.

Similar to the previous night, the dinner provides much food for thought, especially as Nick was not the only one who brought his friends along. Some people decide to leave afterwards and the rest head out to dance the night away at a new club. They had already signed up using a free guest list service to get in early, skip the queue a get discounted entry.

On Sunday morning, Nick meets some of his friends at their favourite brunch restaurant with copies of various newspapers and magazines, discussing everything from current affairs to economics and showbiz news. In the afternoon he hits the gym then enjoys a relaxing session in the sauna, an ideal time to reflect on the past few days and prepare for the week ahead. In the evening he catches up with e-mails and Facebook messages, checks that he is ready for tomorrow's work schedule, and watches a DVD with his girlfriend.

Two years on, Nick achieves a First class degree, and has racked up some awesome work experience. His experiences from his Washington, DC internship led to writing an article in The Times, helped him land another internship at the Foreign Office, and he chooses to work for a multinational consultancy upon graduating, with a £35k starting salary.

17.2 Common excuses

The two stories above illustrate a fundamental fact about leisure – the way you spend it, and the resulting lifestyle, have a significant influence on what is often, wrongly, seen as a completely different, separate part of your life. Why then, do most people spend their leisure in a way that is detrimental to their Four Accounts?

Firstly, let's address one obvious criticism. Some of you may now feel insulted and/or say that we are looking down on the way normal teenagers or twenty-somethings like to spend their time. Here is the problem. If this were truly the way young people consciously wanted to, and enjoyed, spending their time, we would not say a word. But that is not the case, at least judging by the number of our friends who, upon nursing their hangover on a Saturday morning, proclaim that they promise never to do this to themselves ever again. Anything that one regrets afterwards can hardly be classified as a good way of spending your leisure time.

There is a fundamental difference between enjoying something because it is in your comfort zone, and enjoying something because you truly enjoy the act of doing so. We are in many ways subject to the same Newtonian Laws as all other physical objects, in particular the First Law of Inertia. This law is often simplified as *"A body persists in its state of rest or of uniform motion unless acted upon by an external unbalanced force"*.

The same law is surprisingly accurate when applied to people, and in particular the way we spend our leisure time. We are creatures of habit, and unless you make a conscious effort to change this, you will remain inside your comfort zones and continue doing whatever you have been doing in the past. Unfortunately, whatever we have been doing in the past is often not the best way of spending our leisure time. Many of us believe that we would enjoy trying some new activities – we just never actually get down to trying them.

Everyone says they would love to learn a language, start playing an instrument, pick up a sport or some exercise activities, take an evening course, learn to paint or sing and so on. But there is always an excuse to hide behind – they do not have enough time, enough money, there are no opportunities to do such activities near their home, they would need to start getting up earlier or going to sleep later and so on.

Most of these excuses are complete and utter rubbish. The same people who do not have £30 for a painting class will easily splash £60 on dinner and a few overpriced cocktails. The same people who do not have four hours a week to learn playing the violin spend two hours every evening watching TV with no particular interest. The same people who cannot stay up later to attend evening classes have no problems with staying up late to browse the internet without any particular purpose. And the list goes on. Lack of imagination, lack of confidence, lack of leadership – they are all just excuses.

Changing your habits, picking up a new activity and changing your schedule require energy and effort. Sticking to old routines and going clubbing require you to follow the herd. The effort is definitely different, but then so are the payoffs. Jedi Master Yoda said "Do, or do not. There is no try." Stop saying "I would like to …", learn how to say "I am …".

Key Takeaways: Productive Leisure

- 'Leisure' is usually used to describe things that are bad for us, or to put it another way, things that do not increase the Four Accounts.

- The outperformer must correct the environmental and sociological reasons and biases that make him or her spend their leisure time in an unproductive way i.e. one that does not actually produce happiness.

- The two examples illustrate that small differences in your behaviour during your leisure can have a big impact on your lifestyle and career.

- Learn how to make the distinction between enjoying something because it is in your comfort zone, and enjoying something because you truly enjoy the act of doing it. Then adjust your leisure activities accordingly. Do not hide behind excuses.

Don't forget the previous chapter: Thinking Outside the Box

- Thinking outside the box means thinking unconventionally, differently or from an entirely new perspective. It is the ability to ignore or bypass traditional restrictions and barriers, and come up with answers and solutions that are not immediately obvious and arise from non-obvious thought patterns.

- It is difficult to describe and structure something that is by definition hard to replicate. Nevertheless, there are a number of things you can do and techniques you can adopt in order to increase the chances of stumbling upon a good idea.

- Learn how to come up with good questions. This is a key skill for innovation and effective decision making. Knowing the right questions is the first step to knowing the right answers.

- Thinking outside the box can provide some questions that directly help to improve your own decision making about your life – make use of them.

Conclusion

First and foremost, congratulations. Congratulations for taking responsibility for your development to the extent of not just buying this book, but reading to the end. We understand that it is not a simple task – you probably felt quite uneasy at certain points. Perhaps we talked about something that is a sensitive issue to you, or hinted at a mistake you made, and have not squared with yourself. This is all a part of the journey, and we appreciate that you have stayed with us.

Now it is important to understand that this really is just the beginning – although that is probably not what you wanted to hear right now! Excellence is not an event; it is an ongoing process, with all of its ups and downs, losses and victories, easy and difficult parts. We have tried to give you solid foundations, inspire you and get you started in your own race to excellence. Follow the advice of the greatest athletes – take things one step at a time, and make sure that the next one is the best you can do.

Remember too that you are not on your own. We have encouraged you to find friends, partners, mentors and buddies who share your ideals, and who will support you – and expect the same – going forward. We want to re-iterate this advice. We hope to continue helping you with the challenges ahead, and have set up a website for this purpose at www.racing-towards-excellence.com. Further information is at the back of this book. If you have any feedback, thoughts or suggestions, we would like to hear from you at feedback@racing-towards-excellence.com.

Afterword by Muzaffar Khan

This book is a milestone in my journey. I feel that I have crossed the Rubicon and can never go back to putting my passion and happiness second to other considerations. The joy and relief I feel right now, from reaching this plateau, will always act as the inspiration to helping others to a similar state of wellbeing. I feel doubly blessed because as well as helping me, this book is a tool to help others lead balanced and fulfilled lives.

My life has not been a straight line of balanced success but a journey of peaks and troughs. I actually failed my first year in my undergraduate course at the London School of Economics. That was a tough moment because until then I had never experienced failure. However I bounced back to not only do well in my degree but to also gain two further postgraduate degrees. The failure taught me to always treasure my academic achievements and never stop doing my best. I am not suggesting that you should proactively court failure as a route to improvement but if you stumble, as I did, always focus on the learning opportunity in that failure rather than on attacking yourself.[107]

We are all different. It is inevitable that some of us do better in some areas and others excel in a different field. Never get disheartened if you feel that others are doing better than you. It will almost always be the case that you are comparing in a narrow area and over a small period of your life. While we must not allow a decrease in any account, the richness of life is that we have health, wealth, love, inner peace and so many other areas in which we can grow. The greatest harm we do to ourselves is use comparison criteria that are self attacking. Just do your best in the area that you are enjoying working on most now and over time you will choose other areas to strengthen. The speed of your improvement will also vary over time relative to others and that is also ok. When I was 28 I was still a relatively junior currency trader at Barclays Capital and 7 years behind some of my friends from university. But I had picked up all sorts of other skills which meant that by the time I was 33 I had caught up with the very best of my LSE class.

Understanding the theory and then implementing the strategies of this book will change you as a person. Be prepared. In my own life many of the friends I had when I failed my first year at university are no longer in touch. Over the last few years many others have drifted away as I no longer share their interests. That was really tough on me as I was a people pleaser. I have had to learn that personal integrity to my own values must always come before pleasing others. My transition to personal integrity was painful but your shift can be smoother. The key is not to mourn those you lose as you evolve but always be actively looking for new friends who share the values that make you feel good about yourself.

The more dedicated I become to implementing this book the more opportunities and people come into my life that help me to achieve greater and greater happiness and success. What is also remarkable is how many old dysfunctional relationships are changing to loving relationships. It really allows me to see that it takes two to tango.

Discovering a truth and living it day in and day out are two very different challenges. My students are my greatest inspiration to daily practise the strategies outlined in this book. Their dedication to implementing these strategies constantly drives me to raise my own game.

I want to emphasise that where I am is still a plateau and not the peak. The wonderful thing is that there is no limit in your life to the possible amount of happiness and success. That discovery is one of the most valuable truths that I can convey to all of you.

One of my fervent wishes is that while we have written this book as an optimal roadmap for 18–25 year olds, readers of all ages will be able to derive the benefits of leading a life focused on the Four Accounts. To the older readers I want to say that the race towards excellence can start at any stage of your life. I didn't even know that a happiness and success orientated life was the most desirable outcome until I was in my thirties. In my forties I am still racing towards excellence and I hope, regardless of age, you will join me.

Muzaffar Khan
muzaffar@racing-towards-excellence.com

Afterword by Jan Sramek

"The question isn't who is going to let me; it's who is going to stop me."

Ayn Rand, philosopher and novelist

The worst thing about growing up is that you realise how many mistakes you made. The second worst thing is realising that if you knew back then what you know today, perhaps you could have been somewhere else in life. *What would be the one message I would send to my younger self, if I were given the chance?* I often wondered about this in the past; my views on the subject used to change frequently with my own development.

They don't anymore. For the first time in my life, the answer wouldn't change. If I were speaking to my younger self of any age, to my older self of any age, or anyone who asks me for life advice, I'd pass on the quote above.

There are over six and half billion people on this planet. Whatever dream you have, however difficult, unattainable, impossible or outright crazy it may seem, you probably only need 20 of them to buy into your vision and support you in order to make it happen. As for the other six and a half billion, they won't stop you.

The only responsibility you have towards others is to respect their rights. Beyond that, so what that they think you're crazy? What's the worst that could happen? You are the one and only person responsible for your own happiness.

One of the toughest challenges, but greatest rewards, for any perfectionist comes from accepting, rather than just understanding, that the past does not matter. I always understood this logically, but accepting it emotionally took me a very a long time. I have, eventually.

Stop worrying about "what if…?", the opportunities you missed and the mistakes you made. One of my strongest beliefs is in the greatness of man and what he or she can achieve, regardless of the starting point. The distance you have already travelled is irrelevant; what matters is the speed that you gain and sustain from now onwards.

In my own sprint towards excellence, I am barely out of the starting blocks. I have shared with you what has made it possible for me to qualify for the race, but that's just a beginning. I know no purer form of happiness than that which stems from doing great work. I intend to get as much of it as I can in life. I am going to move the boundaries of what is possible in everything I do, and have a ball whilst doing it.

Apple's advert once said *"The people who are crazy enough to think they can change the world are the ones who do."*

Go and make something awesome of your life. Whatever you do, do it for the right reasons. Never stop thinking. Good luck.

Jan Sramek
jan@racing-towards-excellence.com

Acknowledgements

This book is a product of our life experience; it would not have been possible without the innumerable life lessons we have received in the past from our families, teachers, tutors, managers, colleagues, mentors, mentees, buddies, friends and partners. We have been fortunate to have interacted with many individuals who excelled in their fields, and remain grateful for everything we have learnt from them.

Certain people deserve special thanks for their continuing support of this book. Anjool Malde edited the first draft, and together with Ben Lu, provided us with ongoing feedback and ideas. Cong Cong Bo, Corentin Roux dit Buisson, Peter Harrison, Mengyi He, Veronika Kapustina, Daria Kuznetsova, Petra Posnikova, Fay Hanrahan Russell and Sarju Shah have reviewed and commented on the manuscript. Lian Po Kor has been instrumental in the research for this book and subsequent referencing. Lukas Frelich type set the text despite our impossible deadlines.

There are a few people we would like to thank from our *Alma Mater*, the London School of Economics, who have been highly supportive of our work, including Chris Connelley, Drucilla Daley, Beverley Friedgood, Sue Redgrave, Claire Sanders and Fiona Sanford. We are very grateful to Sir Howard Davies for writing the foreword, help and encouragement.

The biggest thank you goes to Owen Roberson, our editor. We have lost count of the number of times when Owen surprised us with his thoughtful comments and suggestions. He has been invaluable in bringing out clarity in our work.

Needless to say, any mistakes that remain are ours alone.

Send us your story!

Do you have experience with implementing any of the ideas in this book? Have you made the mistakes we talk about before? Would you like to tell us about how reading the ideas in this book changed your perspective or life in general?

Personal examples are a powerful way of sharing experience and learning, and we would very much like to hear from you. If you feel that yours or someone else's story might inspire others, and would like to submit it for possible inclusion in a future book, please e-mail it to stories@racing-towards-excellence.com.

Visit our website

Our website (www.racing-towards-excellence.com) is a living continuation of the work we have done in this book. We will be publishing relevant examples and stories, best practices, extensions of our theories and other useful ideas on our blog. More and above, we have established a discussion board where you can share your experiences with others, and learn from their own best practices. There is also a section for further recommended reading, links to other online resources about personal development, useful spreadsheets (including the personal time matrix) and much more.

Appendix A

The following information is taken verbatim from the United Nations Educational, Scientific and Cultural Organization (UNESCO) website.*

Depending on the topic, socio-cultural context, age group etc., the specific life skills needed for an individual at a certain moment and context vary enormously, and it is therefore not possible to draw up a definitive list of essential life skills. There are, however, some cognitive, personal and interpersonal life skills that are generally considered particularly important.

Learning to know – Cognitive abilities

Decision making/problem solving skills

- Information gathering skills
- Evaluating future consequences of present actions for self and others
- Determining alternative solutions to problems
- Analysis skills regarding the influence of values and attitudes of self and others on motivation

Critical thinking skills

- Analyzing peer and media influences
- Analyzing attitudes, values, social norms and beliefs and factors affecting these
- Identifying relevant information and information sources

Learning to be – Personal abilities

Skills for increasing internal locus of control

- Self esteem/confidence building skills
- Self awareness skills including awareness of rights, influences, values, attitudes, strengths and weaknesses
- Goal setting skills
- Self evaluation / Self assessment / Self-monitoring skills

Skills for managing feelings

- Anger management
- Dealing with grief and anxiety
- Coping skills for dealing with loss, abuse, trauma

Skills for managing stress

- Time management
- Positive thinking
- Relaxation techniques

Learning to live together – Inter-personal abilities

Interpersonal communication skills

- Verbal/Nonverbal communication
- Active listening
- Expressing feelings; giving feedback (without blaming) and receiving feedback

Negotiation/refusal skills

- Negotiation and conflict management
- Assertiveness skills
- Refusal skills

Empathy

- Ability to listen and understand another's needs and circumstances and express that understanding

Cooperation and Teamwork

- Expressing respect for others' contributions and different styles
- Assessing one's own abilities and contributing to the group

Advocacy Skills

- Influencing skills and persuasion
- Networking and motivation skills

Though this list suggests that the three categories of skills are distinct from each other, health behaviour typically requires the use of a combination of skills simultaneously. For example, to avoid early pregnancy a young woman may need decision-making skills (*"what are my options?"*), values clarification skills (*"what is important to me?"*), self-management skills (*"how can I protect myself / how can I achieve my goals"*) and interpersonal skills (*"how do I resist pressure to have sex and communicate my decision to others?"*). Ultimately, the interplay between the skills is what produces powerful behavioural outcomes.

---

* http://portal.unesco.org/education/en/ev.php-URL_ID=36637&URL_DO=DO_TOPIC&URL_SECTION=201.html

References

We refer to a number of online sources throughout the end-notes. Unfortunately, we have no control over their respective URLs. We have set up an online interface to address this problem, keep the links up to date and help you identify new locations for any of the sources in case they change.

If you cannot access any of the websites we refer to below, please visit http://www.racing-towards.excellence.com/references/ and choose the appropriate endnote number.

Introduction

[1] The text box explanation of life skills is taken verbatim from the UNESCO website. A fuller version of this is in Appendix A.

http://portal.unesco.org/education/en/ev.php-URL_ID=36637&URL_DO=DO_TOPIC&URL_SECTION=201.html

Muzaffar Khan: Reconciliation

[2] Jack Welch is perhaps the best known supporter of similar rules. He is said to have often used it in various variations during his successful leadership of General Electric.

Welch, J., 2005, "Winning: The Ultimate Business How-To Book"

1. The Four Accounts

[3] On emotional health please see the following:

Goleman, D., 1996, "Emotional Intelligence: Why it Can Matter More Than IQ".

Seligman, M., 2002, "Authentic Happiness".
http://www.authentichappiness.sas.upenn.edu/Default.aspx

Hills, P., and Argyle, M., 2001, "Emotional stability as a major dimension of happiness", Personality and Individual Differences, Volume 31, Number 8, December.

⁴ On material health please see:

Essay by Manel, B., Rakesh, S., 2007, "Does More Money Buy You More Happiness?" in the book "Decision Modeling and Behavior in Complex and Uncertain Environments" Kugler, Tamar; Smith, J. Cole; Connolly, Terry; Son, Young-Jun. Springer New York.

Leonardo, B., 2007, "Does Money Affect Happiness and Self-Esteem? The poor borrowers' perspective in a natural environment", Tor Vergata University CEIS Working Paper Series.

Layard, R., 2007, Happiness: Lessons from a New Science, Penguin.

Layard, R., 2003, "Income and Happiness: Rethinking Economic Policy", London School of Economics Lionel Robbins Memorial Lectures. http://cep.lse.ac.uk/events/lectures/layard/RL040303.pdf

Newsweek, "Why Money Doesn't Buy Happiness", 15 October 2007. http://www.newsweek.com/id/43884

Gardner, J., and Oswald, A.J., 2006, "Money and Mental Wellbeing: A Longitudinal Study of Medium-Sized Lottery Wins", Institute for the Study of Labor (IZA) Discussion Paper Series. ftp://repec.iza.org/RePEc/Discussionpaper/dp2233.pdf

⁵ For mental health see:

Paper by Lu, L., Shih, J.B., 1997, „Personality and happiness: Is mental health a mediator?" in "Personality and Individual Differences" Volume 22, Issue 2, February 1997, Pages 249-256 http://www.sciencedirect.com/science/journal/01918869

Paper by Vaillant, G. "Mental Health", American Journal of Psychiatry, August 2003. pages 1373-1384.

⁶ For Physical health see:

"Physical Activity Fundamental To Preventing Disease" U.S. Department of Health & Human Services June 20, 2002. Specifically the paper states that good physical health "Promotes psychological well-being." http://aspe.hhs.gov/health/reports/physicalactivity/

Dr. Jeff Cherubini of Manhattan College provides an audio exposition "Authentic Happiness through Physical Activity" see:

http://www.healthrelatedfitness.org/home/2008/10/10/episode-10-authentic-happiness-through-physical-activity/

[7] Frank, R., 1999, Luxury Fever: Why Money Fails to Satisfy in an Era of Excess, N.Y. Free Press.

[8] See the global charity Oxfam's work in particular in this area. "We believe that poverty is not inevitable, it is an injustice: it can be tackled." http://www.oxfam.org/

[9] The physical cost on Wall Street individuals is examined by Carin Gorrell in her article "Wall Street Warriors", Psychology Today, Jan/Feb 2001.

http://www.psychologytoday.com/rss/pto-20010101-000010.html

[10] Daniel H. Pink, 2006, "A Whole New Mind: Why Right-Brainers Will Rule the Future"

[11] Arana, J., and Leon, C., 2007, "Do emotions matter? Coherent preferences under anchoring and emotional effects", Ecological Economics, Volume 66, Issue 4.

[12] http://www.msnbc.msn.com/id/25332025/

[13] Schroeder, A., 2008, "The Snowball: Warren Buffett and the Business of Life."

[14] For an article about how Buffett donated a sizeable part of his fortune to the Gates Foundation see: http://news.cnet.com/Buffett-donates-his-billions-to-Gates-foundation/2100-1022_3-6087682.html

[15] Colleen A. Sexton. 2004. "Arnold Schwarzenegger."

[16] World Database of Happiness: http://www1.eur.nl/fsw/happiness/

For alternative conceptualizations and measurements of happiness, see Martin Seligman's Authentic Happiness Project at http://www.authentichappiness.sas.upenn.edu/Default.aspx

For an exposition of happiness from a social science, rather than a psychological perspective, see the first of Lord Richard Layard's 2003 Lionel Robbins Memorial Lectures at the London School of Economics: "What is happiness? Are we getting happier?" at http://cep.lse.ac.uk/events/lectures/layard/RL030303.pdf

Ryff, C., 1989, "Happiness is everything, or is it? Explorations on the meaning of psychological well-being", Journal of Personality and Social Psychology, Vol. 57, No. 6.

Subramaniam, V., 2005, "Management and Development of Happiness: A Priority in Socio-Economic Development", Author's web pages. This paper can be found at http://129.3.20.41/eps/pe/papers/0501/0501008.pdf

[17] For examples of connections between the individual accounts.

Article by Fredrickson, B. "Cultivating Positive Emotions to Optimize Health and Well-being" in Prevention and Treatment, volume 3, 2000. http://www.unc.edu/peplab/publications/cultivating.pdf

FamilyDoctor.org gives a good explanation of how the emotional and physical accounts are connected: "Mind/Body Connection: How Your Emotions Affect Your Health". See: http://familydoctor.org/online/famdocen/home/healthy/mental/782.html

Lerner, J., Small, D., and Loewenstein, G., 2003, "Heart strings and Purse strings: Carryover Effects of Emotions on Economic Decisions", Psychological Science, Volume 15, Number 5. http://mktg-sun.wharton.upenn.edu/ideas/pdf/Small/endowment.pdf

Mind, a leading mental health charity in the UK, on the interrelationships between the material and mental accounts: "Money and Mental Health". http://www.mind.org.uk/money/mentalhealth/mhandyourmoney.htm

BBC, "Money Worries 'may harm health', 8 September 2008. http://news.bbc.co.uk/1/hi/health/7603617.stm

[18] To emphasise the importance of these accounts Muzaffar originally also called them the four pillars of our success in his original series of lectures to the students at the London School of Economics.

2. Inspiration

[19] Maclean, P.D., 1990, "The triune brain in evolution: role in paleocerebral functions".

[20] Gardner, H., 2003, "Multiple Intelligences After Twenty Years", Paper presented at the American Educational Research Association. http://www.pz.harvard.edu/PIs/HG_MI_after_20_years.pdf

[21] An animation of the position of the frontal lobes in the brain can be seen at
http://www.neuroskills.com/tbi/bfrontal.shtml

[22] Zohar D. and Marshall I. 2001 "SQ: Connecting With Our Spiritual Intelligence", The authors define spiritual intelligence as follows:

"By SQ [spiritual quotient] I mean the intelligence with which we address and solve problems of meaning and value, the intelligence with which we can place our actions and our lives in a wider, richer, meaning-giving context, the intelligence with which we can assess that one course of action or one life-path is more meaningful than another. SQ is the necessary foundation for the effective functioning of both IQ and EQ. It is our ultimate intelligence."

[23] Goldberg, E., 2002, "The Executive Brain: Frontal Lobes and the Civilized Mind."

[24] An example of a study that shows how fear is stronger motivator to get fit than hope for those worrying about their bodies can be found at
http://www.bath.ac.uk/news/2007/11/27/gym-fear.html

[25] Giovannoli, J., 2000, "The Biology of Belief: How our biology biases our beliefs and perceptions"

[26] However some sweatshop managers have just got better at hiding abuses. Excellent Business week magazine article (Nov 27, 2006) on this:
http://www.businessweek.com/magazine/content/06_48/b4011001.htm

[27] Sadistic people, on the other hand, are known to derive pleasure from inflicting pain and suffering on others. Given that until recently it was considered a personality disorder, the writers do not see sadistic behaviour as a healthy way to interact with others. See
http://pn.psychiatryonline.org/cgi/content/full/37/13/14

[28] Thrash, T.M., Elliot, A.J., 2004, "Inspiration: core characteristics, component processes, antecedents, and function", Journal of Personality and Social Psychology, Vol. 87, No. 6.

Hymer, S., 1990, "On Inspiration", The Psychotherapy Patient, Volume 6, Issue 3 & 4.

Knowlson, T.S., 1922, "The Psychology of Inspiration", The Psychoanalytic Review, No. 9.

[29] "Thoughts on Google's 20% time"
http://www.scottberkun.com/blog/2008/thoughts-on-googles-20-time/

30 "Give the proper tools to a group of people that want to make a difference, and they will."
    Description of Google's benefit schemes
    http://www.google.com/support/jobs/bin/static.py?page=benefits.html

31 Used widely in the 70/80s in the developed world and still today in many emerging markets who lack the legislation to protect their consumers.

32 Rosenshine, B., Furst, N., 1971, "Research in Teacher Performance Criteria: A Symposium"

33 Bennett, B., 2004, "Year to Success"

34 Edge Foundation, "Michael Phelps ADHD is not an attention deficit", 15 August 2008
    http://www.edgefoundation.org/blog/2008/08/15/michael-phelpss-adhd-is-not-an-attention-deficit/

35 http://www.usatoday.com/sports/golf/sgmast6.htm

36 Booth, N., 2007, "Tiger Traits: 9 Success Secrets You Can Discover from Tiger Woods to Be a Business Champion"

3. Vision

37 Maslow, A.H., 1943, "A Theory of Human Motivation", Psychological Review, 50
    http://chiron.valdosta.edu/whuitt/col/regsys/maslow.html

38 Dr. Russ Dewey provides an exposition of the Freudian view of The Ego at
    http://www.psywww.com/intropsych/ch11_personality/ego.html

39 Monitor on Psychology Volume 37, No. 6 June 2006
    http://www.apa.org/monitor/jun06/burnout.html

40 http://en.wikipedia.org/wiki/Deferred_gratification

41 For a definition and explanation of deferred gratification see
    http://www.nationmaster.com/encyclopedia/Deferred-gratification

    O'Donoghue, T., and Rabin, M., 2000, "The Economics of Immediate Gratification", Journal of Behavioural Decision Making, Volume 13, Issue 2

    Goleman, D., 1996, "Emotional Intelligence: Why it Can Matter More Than IQ."

Mischel, W, 1974, "Processes in Delay of Gratification", Advances in Experimental Social Psychology"

[42] Mischel, W., Shoda, Y., & Rodriguez, M. L. 1989, "Delay of Gratification in Children", Science, Volume 244, Issue 4907, pp. 933-938

[43] Falk, A., and Ichino, A., 2003, "Clean Evidence on Peer Pressure", IZA Discussion Paper No. 732
http://papers.ssrn.com/sol3/papers.cfm?abstract_id=391701

[44] Pavlov, I.P., 1927, Conditioned Reflexes: An Investigation of the Physiological Activity of the Cerebral Cortex

[45] Tseng, M.S., and Carter, A. R., 1970, "Achievement motivation and fear of failure as determinants of vocational choice, vocational aspiration, and perception of vocational prestige", Journal of Counseling Psychology, Vol. 17(2)

http://psycnet.apa.org/index.cfm?fa=main.doiLanding&uid=1970-09309-001

Ramaswami, M., 1998, "How 'carrots and sticks' are encoded in the brain: motivation, reward, addiction and fear", Journal of Biosciences, Volume 23, Number 3
http://www.springerlink.com/content/x103l1362787v600/

[46] Deci, E.L. and Ryan, R.M. (1985) "Intrinsic motivation and self-determination in human behaviour"

4. Love

[47] Freud, S., 1972, "Sexuality and the Psychology of Love".

Peck, M.S., 1978, "The Road Less Traveled: A New Psychology of Love, Traditional Values, and Spiritual Growth"

[48] It is important to note here that we are talking specifically about the mutualism form of symbiotic relationships.
http://www.britannica.com/EBchecked/topic/577677/symbiosis

[49] A quick search on Google for 'how to be liked by everyone' returned more than 42m results.

[50] Freud's idea of the superego is actually quite close to Socrates' idea of "thumos". In both cases there is a desire for recognition by others. For a comparison between the two ideas see Lear J., 2005, "Freud"

[51]   Warren Buffett tops Businessweek's 50 Most Generous Philanthropists
       http://bwnt.businessweek.com/interactive_reports/philanthropy_indi-
       vidual/

[52]   Klass, E.T., Tutin, J.A., 1980, Guilt and Self-Criticism in Depression
       Paper presented at the Annual Meeting of the Eastern Psychological
       Association.

       Blatt, S.J., 1982, "Dependency and self-criticism: Psychological dimen-
       sions of depression", Journal of Consulting and Clinical Psychology, Vol
       50(1)
       http://psycnet.apa.org/index.cfm?fa=main.doiLanding&uid=1982-
       09953-001

5. Responsibility

[53]   Of course, what is missing in this case is the loving intent. According
       to the Stern review, deforestation produces more emissions than the
       transport sector globally.
       http://www.telegraph.co.uk/earth/earthnews/3311141/Scheme-to-stop-
       deforestation-will-pay-for-carbon-not-emitted.html.

[54]   Rachman, S., 1993, "Obessions, Responsibility and Guilt", Behavioural
       Research and Therapy, Volume 31, Issue 2

[55]   Max Weber and charisma
       http://cbae.nmsu.edu/~dboje/teaching/338/charisma.htm

       Flora C. "The X-Factors of Success", Psychology Today, May/Jun 2005
       http://www.psychologytoday.com/articles/pto-20050502-000001.html

6. Measurability and Yardsticks

[56]   For a more detailed look at how to think about balances in accounts see
       also
       Covey, S., 2008, The 7 Habits of Highly Effective Teens

[57]   For more information see http://en.wikipedia.org/wiki/Fosbury_Flop

[58]   Imai, M., 1986, "Kaizen: The Key To Japan's Competitive Success"

7. Habits

[59] Prendergrast, J., Foley, B., Menne, V., and Isaac, A.K., 2008, "Creatures of Habit? The Art of Behavioural Change"
http://www.smf.co.uk/assets/files/publications/SMF_Creatures_of_Habit.pdf

New Scientist, "Why we are all creatures of habit", 4 July 2007
http://www.newscientist.com/article/mg19526111.700-why-we-are-all-creatures-of-habit.html

[60] Stephen Covey's "7 habits of highly effective people" is one of the best books for those wishing to study the subject of habits more thoroughly.

[61] Ted.com video on "Why we know less than ever about the world" by Alisa Miller

http://www.ted.com/index.php/talks/alisa_miller_shares_the_news_about_the_news.html

Davies, N., 2009, Flat Earth News: An Award-winning Reporter Exposes Falsehood, Distortion and Propaganda in the Global Media
an interesting book on the alleged distortion and propaganda in the global media

[62] Social Issues Research Centre, "Social and Cultural Aspects of Drinking", 1998.

http://www.sirc.org/publik/drinking6.html

[63] Those who practise complete abstinence from alcoholic beverages.

[64] Although it is not a topic of this book, neuro-linguistic programming (NLP) has become popular as a way of understanding the power of words on the human psyche.

[65] Soros, G., 1995, "Soros on Soros: Staying Ahead of the Curve"

8. Drive

[66] Hymer, S., 1990, "On Inspiration", The Psychotherapy Patient, Volume 6, Issue 3 & 4.

[67] Harrison, E., 2003, "The 5 Minute Meditator: Quick Meditations to Calm Your Body and Your Mind"

[68] A good example would be meditation – see

http://en.wikipedia.org/wiki/Meditation

[69] Monitor on Psychology, "Probing the depression-rumination cycle", 10 November 2005
http://www.apa.org/monitor/nov05/cycle.html

Bringle M., 1996 "I just can't stop thinking about it: Depression, Rumination, and Forgiveness"
http://www.luthersem.edu/word&world/Archives/16-3_Forgiveness/16-3_Bringle.pdf

[70] *"Neural pathways that are stimulated by the environment and exercised become stronger and larger..on the other hand, neural pathways that are not stimulated or exercised atrophy and die."*
from "Understanding child maltreatment: an ecological and developmental perspective?" by Maria Scannapieco, Kelli Connell-Carrick – Social Science – 2005, page 57

"The more often a neural pathways is used, the stronger it becomes, and the easier it is to trigger. As disused circuits fade away, and with them the promise to more diverse thoughts and talents..."
from "Visual intelligence: perception, image, and manipulation in visual communication?" by Ann Marie Barry. Psychology 1997, page 64

"As we learn, pathways within the brain are created. Without continued use, these pathways decay and you forget. The more often a pathway is used, the stronger the pathway becomes and the easier it is to retrive the stored information. A primary purpose of education is to create new pathways and to reinforence those pathways to make them less suscpetible to decay through repeated use."
from Fostering Retention in Adult Learners, Dr Linda Eagle

[71] A neural pathway is a neural tract connecting one part of the nervous system with another, usually consisting of bundles of elongated, myelin-insulated neurons, known collectively as white matter. Neural pathways serve to connect relatively distant areas of the brain or nervous system, compared to the local communication of grey matter.

[72] Ellen Norman, "Stop blaming others – Get more chances for a calmer and fuller life"
http://ezinearticles.com/?Stop-Blaming-Others---Get-More-Chances-For-a-Calmer-and-Fuller-Life&id=1627591

9. Doing What You Love

[73] Ted.com video on "Why are we happy? Why aren't we happy?" by Daniel Gilbert
http://www.ted.com/index.php/talks/dan_gilbert_asks_why_are_we_happy.html

[74] Paul Buchheit's blog.
http://paulbuchheit.blogspot.com/2009/01/overnight-success-takes-long-time.html

[75] Toltec Tradition
http://www.miguelruiz.com/index.php?option=com_content&view=section&layout=blog&id=1&Itemid=2

10. Health and Fitness

[76] Depression Causes by depression-guide.com
http://www.depression-guide.com/depression-causes.htm

[77] Monitor on Psychology, "Impulsiveness, sensation-seeking characterize the caffeine-dependent", 8 September 2005.
http://www.apa.org/monitor/sep05/impulsiveness.html

Holford, P., 2007, "New Optimum Nutrition for the Mind"

Price M. "Caffeine's wake-up call", Monitor on Psychology, April 2008. See: http://www.apa.org/monitor/2008/04/caffeine.html

[78] "Sleep Is As Important As Diet And Exercise (Only Easier!)"
http://www.medicalnewstoday.com/articles/40294.php

[79] Nutrition 102: Furthering "Eat Real Food"
http://lifespotlight.com/health/2008/06/18/nutrition-102-furthering-eat-real-food/

[80] "Hydration strategies for ultimate energy: how water helps keep your performance afloat"
http://findarticles.com/p/articles/mi_m1608/is_7_18/ai_88583527/

[81] Drewnoski, A., 1997, "Taste preferences and food intake" Annual Review of Nutrition, Vol 17.

[82] Scientific American, "Multiple Studies Confirm Importance of Good Sleep", 14 June 2007.
http://www.scientificamerican.com/podcast/episode.cfm?id=26BE931D-E7F2-99DF-3794A658FDD1BE9D

Scientific American, "To Get Good Grades, Get Good Sleep", 8 December 2008.
http://www.scientificamerican.com/podcast/episode.cfm?id=to-get-good-grades-get-good-sleep-08-12-08

[83] Holford, P., 2004, "The Optimum Nutrition Bible: The Book You Have to Read If You Care About Your Health"

[84] Carr A., 2004, "Positive Psychology: The Science of Happiness and Human Strengths"

[85] Buzan, T., 2003, "The Power of Physical Intelligence: 10 Ways to Tap into your Physical Genius"

[86] Mehrabian, A., 2007, "Nonverbal Communication"

[87] Arts Council UK, "Dance and Health: The Benefits for People of all Ages"
http://www.artscouncil.org.uk/documents/publications/phpNoGNFD.pdf

12. Relationships and Networking

[88] Harford, T., 2008, "The Logic of Life: The Rational Economics of an Irrational World"

[89] Casnocha, B., 2007, "My Start-up Life"

[90] Ferrazzi, K., and Raz, T., 2005, "Never Eat Alone: And Other Secrets to Success, One Relationship at a Time".

[91] Psychology Today, The Science of Laughter, Nov/Dec 2000.
http://www.psychologytoday.com/articles/index.php?term=20001101-000036&page=4

Psychology Today, Laughter: The Best Medicine, 5 April 2005.
http://www.psychologytoday.com/articles/pto-3726.html

[92] Dale Carnegie, "How to win friends and influence people".

14. Racing Against Time

[93] Allen, D., 2002, "Getting Things Done: How to Achieve Stress-free Productivity"

[94] There are a growing number of successful people who argue that one should not check e-mails in the morning, and leave the first processing of inbox until lunchtime or so. If your profession allows you to try such luxury, it may be beneficial to do so.

Morgenstern J., 2005 "Never Check Email in the morning: And other unexpected strategies for making your life work."

[95] Most developed countries have a life expectancy of around 80 years today. Five year olds are nowadays frequent computer and mobile phone users. Assuming that the child born today spends 75 years of their life typing, 365.25 days a year, and types 5000 characters a day (about 1.5 pages of text), they will type 136,968,750 characters in their lifetime. These estimates are all on the conservative side.

15. Study Skills

[96] OECD Programme for International Student Assessment (2003).

[97] I [Jan] remain grateful to teachers and members of staff at Bootham who made this possible.

[98] The Advanced Level General Certificate of Education, universally referred to as an A-Level, is a qualification typically taken between the ages of 16 and 18 in the United Kingdom and some other countries around the world. It is normally considered equivalent to various European and International Baccalaureates, German Abitur or American Advanced Placements.

[99] This excludes the 0/100 I scored on my Decision Mathematics 2 paper. One could score 5*100 = 500 points on 5 papers, guaranteeing an A grade which required 80%*600 = 480 points. I scored enough marks on my previous 5 papers and did not think very highly of the D2 syllabus, so handed in a blank answer sheet and left the exam.

[100] Gladwell, M., 2008, "Outliers: The Story of Success".

[101] Albert Einstein: "The intuitive mind is a sacred gift and the rational mind is a faithful servant. We have created a society that honors the servant and has forgotten the gift."

Stephen Hawking's intuitive approach to subjects that are otherwise beyond comprehension for most people is another testimony to this principle. See

Hawking, S., 2008, "A Brief History of Time"

16. Thinking Outside the Box

[102] It is meant to have originated within the Walt Disney Company, where the puzzle was used in-house. More information about its creator can be seen at http://www.creativethinkingassoc.com/mikevance.html

[103] Johansson, F., 2004, "The Medici Effect: Breakthrough Insights at the Intersection of Ideas, Concepts, and Cultures "

See also the author's website:

http://www.themedicieffect.com/book/book.html

[104] One of the Greek tribes made everyone learn an instrument for this reason.

[105] "How to generate inspiration on demand"
http://veryevolved.com/2009/01/how-to-generate-inspiration-on-demand/

[106] "How Twitter can make you a better and happier person"
http://blogs.zappos.com/blogs/ceo-and-coo-blog/2009/01/25/how-twitter-can-make-you-a-better-and-happier-person

and "5 thought experiments that might change your life"
http://calnewport.com/blog/2009/01/22/5-thought-experiments-that-might-change-your-life/

Afterword by Muzaffar Khan

[107] An excellent book on this subject is "Peaks and Valleys: making good and bad times work for you – at work and in life" by Spencer Johnson, M.D. 2009.